# COCKROACH MANIFESTO FOR AI WINTER

How the Despised Outlast the Unicorn:

*A Business Survival Manual*

A Book in the Gods Must Be Crazy Series

SAJI MADAPAT

Publisher: Tiger Rider



This is a work of nonfiction. Contemporary events, active proceedings, and dated statistics are identified in the notes. The frameworks are diagnostic heuristics, not legal, financial, medical, engineering, or investment advice.

*Proceeds from this book will be donated to the Mother Teresa Mission (Missionaries of Charity) or similar missions.*

# Contents

# I Am a Cockroach

. . .

Jantar Mantar, New Delhi. June 2026. Forty degrees before noon, and the monsoon still owes the city a month of rain.

A twenty-year-old named Saloni Taneja has not slept. She is holding three things: a rose, a copy of the Constitution of India, and a hand-lettered sign that says I AM A COCKROACH.

Three weeks ago, the Chief Justice of India looked down from the highest bench in the republic and described people like her—the young, the jobless, the ones the examinations keep failing on purpose—as cockroaches. Parasites of society. People who, denied a place in the professions, become "activists" and start attacking everyone.

He had a gavel, a Constitution of his own, and the full weight of the state behind him, and he reached for the vocabulary of an exterminator.

The next day he explained that he had been misunderstood.

The internet had already taken custody of the word.

Within twenty-four hours, a strategist with a phone and no budget had founded a political party for the insulted and posted the eligibility criteria: unemployed, lazy, chronically online, and able to rant professionally. Three million people joined in seventy-eight hours. They printed the slur on T-shirts. They cut it into masks. They carried it here, to the old observatory where Delhi has always come to measure things—first the stars, now the distance between a government and its children.

By the time the monsoon breaks, the insult will have more than twenty million followers. The police will answer roses with tear gas and count their own damage in the hundreds. An education minister will resign. A parliament that could not previously locate the examination system will pass a law about it in four days.

And a Supreme Court justice will have discovered the one thing you must never do to a generation with nothing left to lose.

You must never give it a name.

Saloni is not in this book because she is exotic. She is here because she has a colleague you have already met: the mid-level manager watching an "AI efficiency program" become a quiet layoff list; the founder whose bridge round was "temporarily reprioritized"; the engineer who maintained the system for nine years and was let go because nothing ever went wrong. Same species. Different lighting.

The powerful keep reaching for the same insult, and the insult keeps meaning the same thing: *we have already tried to remove you, and we have already failed.*

You must never give a generation a name it can wear.

This is a book about business.

Stay with me. Your organization has more in common with Saloni than with the judge who named her.

*Because if you do not understand why a twenty-year-old in a tear-gas cloud wearing an insect mask is the ultimate leading indicator for your Q3 earnings, you are already dead.*

Your executive dashboard measures click-through rates. The street measures pitchforks. Only one of these is a lagging indicator.

# The Clock Ran Out. The Cockroach Did Not.

. . .

The clarification was relevant. It was also late. The word had acquired owners.

On May 15, 2026, Chief Justice of India Surya Kant used "cockroaches" and "parasites" during a hearing concerning professional credentials. On May 16, he said sections of the media had misquoted him and that his criticism was aimed at people who entered professions with fake or bogus degrees—not Indian youth generally.[1]

He tried to narrow the meaning the next day.

The internet had already taken custody of the word.

A slur does not report back to its author for operating instructions. Within days, strategist Abhijeet Dipke had founded the Cockroach Janta Party and issued eligibility criteria that read like unemployment had hired a comedy writer: jobless, lazy, chronically online, able to rant professionally. Millions followed. Masks and T-shirts appeared. By June, the comparison had become a street movement over examination failures, unemployment, and public accountability. By late July, the movement declared victory after Education Minister Dharmendra Pradhan resigned and the government announced stronger examination reforms.[2]

The insult had mutated.

Not literally. The internet has done enough damage to evolutionary biology. But the cultural inversion was exquisite. Respectable society reaches for the cockroach to mean dirty, invasive, unwanted, beneath notice, difficult to remove.

The targets heard only the last property: *difficult to remove.*

And do not file this under exotic foreign news. The West has been drying its own tinder since 2008. Call the condition what the evidence supports—not civil war, but a legitimacy aftershock.

The financial system broke. The political system rescued it. Millions of citizens concluded, fairly or not, that capitalism had discovered socialism at precisely the moment the creditors needed it. COVID widened the crack. Inflation taxed people least able to hedge it. War returned energy and industrial capacity to the vocabulary of national security. Then AI arrived to audit the old bargain that education, credentials, and white-collar competence would purchase a stable place in the middle class.

By 2026, only 32 percent of respondents worldwide believed the next generation would be better off. In the United States, 21 percent did—down nine points in a year.[3]

A generation does not become revolutionary because a survey says it is gloomy. History is not a vending machine where you insert distrust and get an uprising. But dry material matters when a spark lands.

There are rebellions built around noble animals: eagles, lions, stallions galloping photogenically into sunsets. Then there is the cockroach. No flag designer has ever stared at one and whispered, *Majestic*. It has no personal brand, no keynote, and no TED Talk called *Finding My Authentic Exoskeleton*.

It simply refuses to cooperate with your preferred ending.

## The clock

Twenty-six years before the insult, Peter Drucker started a clock. In August 2000, he warned that "the corporation as we know it" was unlikely to survive another twenty-five years—" legally and financially, yes, but not structurally and economically."[4]

The Delaware filing survived 2025. So did the Chief Transformation Officer, having transformed mostly the reporting relationships beneath him. But Drucker's deeper target was the twentieth-century design: stable boundaries, deep hierarchies, information scarcity, and managers serving as relays between the people who knew and the people permitted to decide.

Then artificial intelligence arrived carrying a flamethrower and a consulting proposal.

By 2026, Stanford's AI Index reported AI use in at least one function among 88 percent of surveyed organizations, while agent deployment remained in the single digits across nearly all business functions. The technology had colonized the strategy deck faster than it had colonized the operating system.[5]

AI had not abolished the organization. It had made the organization's design defects harder to hide. Where does a company end when suppliers, contractors, customers, open-source communities, models, platforms, and machines all participate in creating what the customer buys? What is the corporation for when intelligence is no longer trapped inside it?

Commentators offered the agile network, the platform, the ecosystem, the decentralized autonomous organization.

I propose an insect.

## The wrong animal

This will upset respectable people. Good. Respectable people already gave us the unicorn as an economic category: an animal that does not exist, cannot reproduce, possesses no known habitat, and is distinguished from an ordinary horse mainly by an implausible object protruding from its forehead. Then they assigned it a billion-dollar valuation and congratulated it for mistaking the thermostat for nature.

And the cockroach is supposed to be the ridiculous metaphor?

The startup world stumbled onto the truth once, then filed it under weather. In late 2008, Airbnb's founders were in debt and nearly out of options, keeping their company alive by hand-folding election-themed cereal boxes. At their Y Combinator interview, Joe Gebbia produced the boxes and explained the stunt. Paul Graham reportedly leaned back and said, "You guys are like cockroaches. You just won't die."[6]

The industry understood the compliment during an investment winter. **When the heat lamps returned, it went back to breeding horses with glue guns.**

Persistence alone is not the doctrine. Bad restaurants persist. Bureaucracies persist. Parasites persist. The relevant difference is structural:

---

*The Unicorn Company is designed to become extraordinary under favorable assumptions.*

*The Cockroach Company is designed so fewer favorable assumptions are necessary.*

---

One requires the future to cooperate. The other assumes the future has not signed the term sheet.

The Unicorn Company is not simply a valuation threshold. It is an operating wager. It assumes capital remains available, intelligence remains scarce, the founder remains central, one dramatic moat remains defensible, scale remains politically tolerable, and an exit window arrives before the obligations mature. None of those assumptions is absurd by itself. Requiring all of them to remain true at once is the design flaw.

## The confession

I know something about the first design because I spent decades inside large transformation programs—helping organizations optimize, standardize, centralize, outsource, automate, and occasionally amputate themselves with immaculate slides. I learned how reported efficiency can rise while institutional competence falls; how a company can look healthier precisely because the organs that would warn it of danger have been removed.

Somewhere in a drawer I keep a thank-you plaque from an engagement that, three years later, had left the client less able to think without outside help. I have never decided whether the plaque is a trophy or a confession. That is why the drawer stays shut.

The Corporate Arsonist in these pages is not a villain standing outside the system. He is a confession from inside it.

The cockroach matters not because small is always beautiful, capital is always corrupt, or disruption is always foolish. It matters because modern management has spent a century asking how an organization can perform brilliantly when its assumptions hold. The urgent question is how to design an organization so fewer assumptions have to hold at all.

This is also where my Camel must molt. The Camel was the necessary rebellion: reserves over theater, patience over blitzscaling, endurance over applause. But the Camel assumes a desert—harsh, scarce, and legible. The Cockroach begins when the map becomes unreliable: desert today, flood tomorrow, data center Tuesday, regulatory tribunal Wednesday, and a bridge round "temporarily reprioritized" on Friday.

---

*The Camel assumes climate. The Cockroach assumes regime change.*

---

The Unicorn assumes a benevolent deity will keep the interest rates at zero and the regulatory agencies asleep. It is an operating model based entirely on divine intervention.

## The spine

The Gods in this book are not supernatural. They are simply institutions large enough to change the weather for everyone else.

One final piece of architecture, stated once and then enacted:

**THE GODS MAKE WEATHER.** States, courts, central banks, markets, platforms, militaries, hyperscalers, and elite institutions can change the environment for everyone beneath them. They need not be malicious. Weather does damage without holding a meeting about it.

**THE WEATHER ENTERS THE ENTERPRISE THROUGH FIVE WINTERS.** Capital. Margin. Productivity. Infrastructure. Legitimacy.

**THE DAMAGE APPEARS IN SIX ORGANS.** Cash. Customers. Compute. Capabilities. Command. Culture.

**The organism either changes shape in time—the molt—or discovers that its strategy was only a sunny-weather costume.**

**And survival earns one final question: was what survived worth inheriting?**

Before learning from the insect, however, we must do something management writers traditionally avoid when a metaphor is performing well.

We must check whether any of it is true.

This is not a book about becoming invincible. Nothing is. It is a book about becoming **difficult to kill for stupid reasons.**

---

*The despised in this book are not a moral caste. They are the people, capabilities, and institutions the dominant system has stopped pricing correctly: young workers, maintainers, local knowledge, small firms, unfashionable crafts, public schools, and communities living beneath somebody else's infrastructure. Contempt is not proof of virtue. It is often evidence that power has stopped listening.*

---

# PART I

## ENTOMOLOGICAL ECONOMICS

. . .

Silicon Valley borrows biology whenever it wants inevitability: ecosystems, viral growth, evolutionary winners, unicorns. The last animal on that list does not exist, but it did come with excellent branding.

This Part returns the compliment with actual entomology.

Companies are not insects. Evolution is not a management philosophy, and nature does not issue ESG reports. But a lineage shaped by reality over immense spans of time has earned the right to cross-examine organizations selected by a three-minute pitch and a favorable interest-rate cycle.

The cockroach's lesson is not invincibility. It is how to fail in pieces rather than all at once: compress without amputating, distribute control without dissolving purpose, change behavior without losing identity, recycle resources, and live inside infrastructure somebody else paid for without forgetting that somebody else owns it.

Before this book enters AI winter, it will submit its mascot to due diligence. If the insect turns out to be a myth, the myth dies here.

A survival doctrine that cannot survive fact-checking deserves the shoe.

# Kill the Nuclear Cockroach

. . .

The cockroach will not survive a nuclear explosion.

Good.

Now we can talk about what actually keeps things alive.

We built an entire resilience myth around the opposite claim because one cinematic superpower is easier to sell than ten boring defenses. In the popular version, humanity completes its long-threatened hostile takeover of itself, the mushroom clouds disperse, and a cockroach emerges to ask whether the abandoned Nvidia GPUs are available at auction.

The biology is less cooperative. In a classic experiment comparing twelve arthropod species exposed to gamma radiation, the American cockroach was the most sensitive species tested. Other arthropods did better. A shoe deployed with sufficient conviction still ends the discussion.[7]

That is not a defect in the metaphor. It is the point.

Resilience is not invulnerability. It begins with an inventory of the ways you can die.

## Its lineage is old because it changed

Cockroaches are often called "living fossils," as though the modern animal spent hundreds of millions of years refusing software updates. Fine copy. Bad evolutionary history.

Cockroach-like fossils reach deep into the Paleozoic, but molecular evidence places the last common ancestor of living cockroaches and termites roughly 235 million years ago, followed by extensive diversification, dispersal, and adaptation. The lineage endured not by discovering one perfect design and embalming it, but by preserving what had to persist while repeatedly changing what did not.[8]

Businesses often reverse that logic. They preserve the org chart and change the mission. Preserve executive incentives and change the employees. Preserve the legacy architecture and change the PowerPoint colors. Evolution has less sentimental attachment to reporting lines.

A long-lived organization must separate identity from implementation.

---

***Endurance = continuity of purpose × capacity for mutation.***

---

All mutation and no continuity produces an identity crisis. All continuity and no mutation produces a museum. Your promise may be ancient. Your machinery must remain young.

## Ten boring defenses beat one glamorous superpower

The American cockroach genome tells a more useful story than nuclear folklore. Researchers found expansions in gene families associated with environmental sensing, chemoreception, detoxification, and other adaptive functions suited to an omnivorous scavenger living in complex urban environments.[9]

There is no single Cockroach Superpower. There is a portfolio. It senses, flees, squeezes, scavenges, detoxifies, changes diet, exploits shelter, and recovers from bad positions.

None deserves a keynote.

Together they make exterminators drink.

The business translation is equally unglamorous: cash, customer diversity, supplier alternatives, portable data, replaceable model providers, direct customer relationships, cross-trained people, documentation, cybersecurity, and the ability to operate in degraded mode. No layer guarantees survival. The value lies in failing differently.

The unicorn wants one extraordinary advantage.

The cockroach wants no ordinary weakness to become fatal.

## Every moat deserves an obituary

When a board announces that its moat is a proprietary AI model, do not applaud. Write the obituary.

What happens when an open model reaches acceptable quality? When a hyperscaler bundles the feature into software the customer already buys? When the model supplier changes its terms? When the customer decides the model matters less than workflow, trust, or accountability?

Your moat does not live outside politics. Washington can restrict the chip. Beijing can subsidize the rival. Brussels can redefine the liability. Delhi can require localization. War can reprice energy. A central bank can reprice the decade. Strategy calls these exogenous shocks, which is economist-speak for 'the weather the slide deck ignored.'

---

*Silicon Valley sells the Holy Moat because it fits on a slide.*

---

The corporate equivalent of a medieval peasant defending a puddle of horse urine because a guy in a fleece vest told him it was an elixir.

A moat, examined honestly, is the interval between the day a thing is hard, and the day it becomes a checkbox in somebody else's product. It is not a body of water. It is a countdown.

A proprietary model dies through convergence or commoditization; own the workflow, context, distribution, and trust above it. One giant customer dies through repricing, acquisition, or procurement change; diversify revenue and modularize the offer. Cheap cloud infrastructure dies through repricing, outage, regulation, or geopolitical restriction; preserve portability and a useful degraded mode.

Every competitive advantage should have a corresponding kill scenario. If management cannot imagine one, management has stopped doing strategy and begun doing theology.

Now run the obituary on the strategy itself. List every condition that must remain true: cheap capital, cheap compute, friendly regulators, a founder who never leaves, a vendor who never reprices, customers who never learn, competitors who never copy, and an exit window that remains open just long enough to flatter the cap table.

Count them.

That is your Miracle Budget.

---

*One miracle may be strategy.*
*Seven miracles is a religion.*
*And venture capitalists make terrible priests.*

---

When your primary competitive advantage is "we rent our brain from Sam Altman slightly faster than you do," you do not have a moat. You have a subscription fee wearing a disguise.

## Build compartments, not prophecies

Most resilience programs ask, "How do we prevent bad things from happening?" Cockroach strategy adds a ruder question: "How do we stop one bad thing from becoming everything?"

A resilient software system does not promise zero defects; it isolates defects. A resilient supply chain does not pretend suppliers never fail; it contains the blast radius. A resilient organization does not promise zero resignations; it prevents one resignation from deleting the institution's memory. A resilient company does not require every product to succeed; it makes product failure survivable.

I have watched executive teams devote enormous attention to reducing the probability of a visible failure while ignoring the architecture that allowed a small failure to cascade. The board discussed prevention. The system had no compartments.

This is the first heresy of the Cockroach Manifesto:

---

*Stop building organizations around superpowers.*
*Build them around failure containment.*

---

## The Molt

A survival doctrine can become a bunker. Cash can become cowardice, redundancy can become bureaucracy, and optionality can become indecision wearing sensible shoes.

Some opportunities deserve concentrated bets. The doctrine is not *never risk death.* It is *knowing what can kill you, and choosing consciously which risks deserve that privilege.*

Unicorn strategy asks what makes defeat impossible. Cockroach strategy asks what makes defeat nonfatal. The first must be right. The second must still be able to learn after being wrong.

> **Cockroach Test**—*What event does your board treat as impossible—and what happens if it occurs next Monday?*

---

*Write the obituary while the moat still has water in it.*

---

# Compressibility Beats Brittle Efficiency

. . .

Place an American cockroach before a horizontal gap smaller than one-quarter of its standing height.

It does not commission a transformation roadmap.

It changes geometry.

In UC Berkeley experiments, cockroaches compressed their bodies by roughly 40 to 60 percent, crossed some crevices in less than a second, continued moving rapidly while confined, and withstood extraordinary forces relative to body weight. The work later inspired a compressible search-and-rescue robot.[12]

The insect does not permanently amputate 40 percent of itself because a benchmark found the body inefficient. It preserves the organism while reducing the space required to operate.

Lean asks: *How little can we operate with?*

Compressibility asks the harder question: *How far can we shrink temporarily without destroying our ability to expand again?*

## Lean removes waste. Brittle efficiency harvests organs.

Genuine Lean practice seeks to remove waste, overburden, and unevenness while building quality into the work. It is not a theological defense of starvation.[13]

Spreadsheet capitalism read Toyota and concluded that the fire extinguishers should go because daily utilization was only 0.003 percent. It removed people, suppliers, inventory, maintenance, training, and institutional memory, then called the fragility "lean."

Lean removes waste.

Brittle efficiency harvests organs.

The test is not whether cost came out. Cost always comes out eventually; bankruptcy is exceptionally committed to the program. The test is whether the organization can become smaller without amputating the capabilities required to recover.

## The Compression Ratio

Suppose revenue falls 30 percent, capital markets close, and the largest customer freezes discretionary spending. You have ninety days.

What portion of operating expense can disappear while the capabilities needed for recovery remain intact?

One software company cuts from ten million dollars a month to seven by dismissing key engineers, eliminating customer success, breaking supplier commitments, and turning the remaining employees into a support group with laptops. Another reaches six and a half million by suspending speculative projects, reducing variable cloud use, freezing expansion hiring, trimming executive compensation, reallocating cross-trained people, and renegotiating contracts designed to flex.

The second company is not merely leaner.

It possesses a different geometry.

*Call the measure the Compression Ratio: the share of operating cost that can be removed within a defined period while preserving the irreducible capabilities required to recover.*

Every fixed commitment should answer a rude question: what happens if we must become half our current size?

Can the real-estate footprint shrink? Can software licenses and cloud use contract? Do debt covenants convert a downturn into an execution? Can expensive features be disabled while the essential service survives? Can the product operate at 80, 60, or 40 percent of ordinary resources without exporting the failure to the customer?

Growth without the capacity to shrink is not scale.

It is swelling.

## Hard shell, soft body

The cockroach's mechanical advantage comes from rigid plates joined by compliant membranes—protection without total rigidity. The organizational doctrine is hard shell, soft body.

The shell contains what must not flex: cybersecurity, safety, financial controls, data integrity, legal obligations, customer promises, ethical red lines, and a quality floor beneath which the company will not descend.

Nearly everything else should remain negotiable: the org chart, titles, meeting rituals, office location, vendor configuration, product packaging, technology provider, hiring plan, and budget allocation.

Many corporations do the reverse. They become soft on ethics and rigid on procedure. They bend the customer promise while treating the reporting structure as Mosaic law.

## Who absorbs the shock?

AI makes the distinction urgent. Suppose a function can operate with 30 percent fewer human hours. The conventional question appears immediately: "Which 30 percent of the people can we remove?"

Sometimes headcount must fall. A manifesto does not become ethical by pretending arithmetic has feelings. But the speed with which management discovers all available elasticity in the people with the least bargaining power is not mathematics. It is hierarchy revealing itself.

Can the saved hours compress cycle time, deepen customer relationships, document tacit knowledge, create backup coverage, improve quality, or build recovery capacity? Or will the company automate the visible labor, delete the invisible immune system, and declare victory before the first unusual case arrives?

There is a special kind of executive genius that fires the people who know why the machine makes that noise, books the savings in Q2, hears the noise in Q4, and hires consultants in Q1 to conduct a root-cause transformation.

*It is the corporate equivalent of selling your own kidney to buy a nicer watch.*

And the most infuriating part? The executive still gets his bonus because "organ harvesting" was listed as a key strategic synergy.

**I know the creature.**

**I used to help design its habitat.**

The first shock absorber should not automatically be the human being with the least leverage. The order matters.

*Flex prestige and vanity first; then speculative programs; duplicated software and infrastructure; executive incentives; and expansion commitments. Human capability comes last—and only after management has priced the loss of memory, trust, and recovery capacity.*

Protect the knowledge, trust, licenses, customer relationships, safety competence, and operating memory required for recovery. Design infrastructure, temporary capacity, discretionary projects, facilities, and outside services to flex. Cut decorative metabolism—vanity programs, duplicative tools, prestige offices, and conferences where adults fly business class to discuss sustainability—with enthusiasm.

The spreadsheet hates unused capacity. Reality is more selective. A second supplier looks inefficient until the first fails. Cross-trained employees look suboptimal until the specialist leaves. Cash looks lazy until credit disappears.

Slack is valuable only when it purchases time, recovery, negotiating leverage, surge capacity, experimentation, or independence. If it purchases nothing, it is fat. If it purchases survival, it is an option.

Every organization compresses. The moral question is what it chooses to crush.

## The Molt

Compressibility can become chronic austerity. If every person is treated as elastic capacity, loyalty becomes irrational; if every quarter begins with "what can we cut?", excellence becomes whatever management has not yet benchmarked out of existence.

Reversible compression is not permanent contraction. **A spring that never recoils is just a bent piece of metal.**

> **Cockroach Test**—*Could you reduce operating burn by one-third within ninety days without destroying the capability, trust, and institutional memory required to recover?*

The crevice is coming for everyone. **Meet it as a spring, not a fracture.**

# Headless, Not Leaderless

. . .

A decapitated cockroach can still execute a directionally appropriate escape turn.

A Fortune 500 employee may be unable to issue a ten-dollar refund without a committee that meets during lunar eclipses.

Only one of these is usually called governance.

The biology is more precise—and more useful—than the folklore. Cockroach locomotor control is distributed through neural structures in the thorax and abdomen rather than residing exclusively in the brain. When researchers removed descending input, the insects still produced appropriate escape turns, although performance degraded. The head mattered. It simply was not required for every leg to know that fire was bad.[14]

## The CEO as nervous-system bottleneck

A customer discovers an unusual problem. The frontline employee knows what happened, and her manager knows how to fix it, but the action falls outside policy.

The manager asks a director, who asks Finance, which asks Legal, which asks Compliance. A briefing deck enters a Steering Committee that meets every second Thursday except during earnings blackout. Six weeks later, a senior vice president authorizes the action proposed on day one.

The company then announces an agile transformation.

This is a nervous system in which the foot must fax the brain, wait for a cross-functional review of the fire, and receive an action item titled *Fire: Next Steps.*

---

*By which point the leg has burned to the knee.*

---

...and the steering committee has scheduled a post-mortem on the ashes, while Legal drafts a memo arguing the knee was technically out of compliance with the dress code anyway.

Which decisions truly require the head? Purpose. Ethical boundaries. Existential resource allocation. Capital structure. System-wide risk. The definition of victory.

Keep those at the center.

But when the environment changes faster than information can climb the hierarchy and permission can descend, centralization becomes a sensory disability.

---

*Centralization is not the existence of a head. It is requiring the head to feel every foot.*

---

The useful measure is **Command Latency**: the interval between reality changing and the person closest to reality being *permitted* to respond.

Not informed.

Not invited to a workshop.

Permitted.

For reversible decisions, that interval should be measured in hours, not pilgrimage stages.

## Founder worship is single-point-of-failure architecture

Founders often carry unusual conviction. They protect missions from institutional mediocrity, move faster than committees, and see opportunities professional managers dismiss.

The problem is not founders.

The problem is an architecture that requires a founder to remain supernatural forever.

We have made "visionary" a job title and succession a form of blasphemy. Strategy lives in one person's intuition. Capital follows one personality. Customer relationships converge on one individual. Employees interpret moods as policy. The company does not possess a culture; it possesses weather around a person.

That is not charismatic leadership.

It is a single point of failure with a podcast.

Succession is not an HR event conducted after the chair turns seventy-three. It is architecture. A leader succeeds when purpose, memory, relationships, and judgment can survive the leader's departure without requiring the successor to perform an impersonation.

## Build a self-righting organization

A better corporate goal than "never fall" is self-righting.

Researchers studying three cockroach species found that they self-righted within thirty seconds in 97 percent of trials, using different combinations of legs, wings, body deformation, pitching, and rolling.[15]

Every company eventually falls over. A major customer disappears. A product launch fails. A supplier collapses. A cyberattack lands. A financing round evaporates. A technical assumption proves false.

The question is not whether the fall occurs. It is how many independent mechanisms can return the organization to viability.

"Raise another round" is not self-righting. It is waiting for someone else to turn you over.

Engineers understand degraded mode. Aircraft, networks, and ships do not need to operate perfectly to remain useful. A company should know the least capable version of itself that can still protect people, serve a customer, and earn revenue without its CEO, primary model vendor, biggest customer, headquarters, preferred marketing channel, or next equity round.

## The Cockroach Constitution

Distributed action requires a clearer center, not a weaker one. A Cockroach Constitution should be shorter than the employee handbook and answer four bitter questions.

*Purpose: What must remain true even when the product, leadership, and technology change?*

*Boundary: What will we refuse even when desperate?*

*Decision rights: Which reversible decisions belong closest to the customer, code, machine, or problem?*

*Escalation: What can threaten the whole organism and therefore must move upward immediately?*

That is hard shell, soft body translated into governance.

The shell is clarity.

The body is autonomy.

## The Molt

Decentralization can become fragmentation. Local teams can optimize against one another, regional autonomy can fracture a brand, and independent technology choices can produce architectural sewage.

The choice is not centralization or decentralization. Centralize the purpose, ethical red lines, existential standards, and shared truth. Distribute reversible action toward reality.

The head matters; it simply should not be required for every leg to know what to do.

The judge left the room. The movement was still in the street at midnight. Headless is not the handicap. Headless is the design.

**Cockroach Test**—*If the CEO vanished for ninety days, what would stop—and why?*

*The leader can leave the room. The purpose cannot. That is the design.*

# Bait Resistance: Your Growth Hack Is Expiring While You Read This

. . .

Somewhere in the history of pest control, somebody had an elegant idea.

Cockroaches like sugar.

Poison kills cockroaches.

Put poison in sugar.

Economics departments would call this incentive alignment.

Cockroaches called it Tuesday.

Then populations of German cockroaches exposed to glucose-containing toxic baits developed heritable glucose aversion. In those insects, glucose did not merely stimulate normal sugar-sensing neurons; it also activated bitter-sensing pathways and suppressed the ordinary sweet response. What once signaled food came to signal danger.[16]

The bait did not merely fail.

The bait trained the market.

## Every growth hack teaches the customer

Business strategy often treats the customer as static. The firm optimizes; the customer receives.

But customers learn what "free" means. They learn where the cancellation button is hidden. They learn that "personalized" often means their first name was inserted into a sequence. They learn that "AI-powered" may be a chatbot placed over a workflow that already worked. Then they resist.

The customer is only the first pupil. Every successful strategy teaches the entire ecosystem how to defeat it. Competitors imitate it. Platforms reprice it. Regulators examine it. Fraudsters industrialize it. Employees game it. Customers simply become less impressed.

A channel works. Marketers find it. Consultants name it. Software automates it. Everyone adopts it. Customers drown in it. Response rates fall. Someone announces that the channel is dead. Six months later, another company raises forty million dollars to build an AI that produces ten times more of the dead thing, faster.

Civilization advances.

Watch the decay rate: response, conversion, referral, retention, willingness to share data, and trust in "AI-assisted" claims. Yesterday's growth engine often becomes today's melting ice cube with a marketing budget.

## Power does not control the afterlife of its insults

Power lays bait too.

On May 15, 2026, Chief Justice of India Surya Kant used "cockroaches" and "parasites" during a hearing while describing people he said attacked institutions. The next day he said the remarks had been misreported and were intended for people who had entered professions through fake or bogus degrees.[1]

But social meaning is not a proprietary asset.

Within weeks, a movement calling itself the Cockroach Janta Party had drawn millions of followers and carried the word into street protests over unemployment, examination failures, and public accountability. The speaker tried to narrow the meaning; the meaning kept moving.[2]

The insult was meant to classify people as beneath consideration.

They retained one feature from the classification: *difficult to remove.*

Power may control the insult.

It does not control the insult's afterlife.

---

*A slur, once released, does not report back to its author for operating instructions.*

---

## Your moat is not the tactic. It is the mutation rate.

The deeper advantage is not a permanent channel, pricing trick, interface, or campaign. It is how quickly the organization discovers that what worked has stopped working.

Not random pivoting. Not logo therapy. Not launching an AI product because the board saw one at Davos.

Useful mutation requires a cheap mechanism for testing variations in channel, pricing, onboarding, product bundle, customer segment, interface, model provider, or cost structure. Ten bounded fifty-thousand-dollar experiments create a different survival profile from one immaculate fifty-million-dollar transformation.

The first produces information.

The second produces a Steering Committee and an incentive not to discover failure.

Let the experiment die, not the company.

## Adaptation sends an invoice

Glucose aversion has costs. On glucose-rich diets, glucose-averse cockroaches showed constrained intake, lower body reserves, and reduced performance relative to wild-type insects. An adaptation valuable under one selection pressure can become a disadvantage when the environment changes again.[17]

Business books prefer superpowers without invoices: become agile, decentralized, diversified, automated, focused, scaled, specialized.

But specialization sacrifices flexibility. Redundancy consumes capital. Speed sacrifices deliberation. Outsourcing buys flexibility at the price of dependence. Vertical integration buys control at the price of fixed cost.

---

*There are no free superpowers.*

*There are only portfolios of trade-offs.*

The objective is not maximum mutation. It is adaptation whose cost remains survivable after the next change in weather.

## AI and the industrial production of bait

Generative AI lowers the marginal cost of personalized messages, advertising variants, synthetic video, sales outreach, political persuasion, and automated follow-up.

When the cost of bait collapses, the supply of bait explodes.

Human attention does not.

The result is an arms race between machine-generated persuasion and human resistance. Spam filters improve. Platforms impose constraints. Consumers become more skeptical. Employees stop believing every message labeled *transformation*. Citizens learn that "authentic grassroots content" occasionally has a media-buying budget and a synthetic jawline.

Advantage migrates toward what remains expensive to manufacture: reputation earned over time, verified identity, credible accountability, communities with memory, and products customers discuss without being bribed by an affiliate link.

*When synthetic persuasion becomes abundant, non-synthetic credibility becomes scarce.*

We have industrialized the production of synthetic bullshit. And we act surprised when the consumer develops a synthetic bullshit allergy. You cannot prompt-engineer trust. You cannot A/B test a soul.

## The Molt

Mutation can become strategy ADHD. Sense constantly; change selectively.

A stable purpose gives tactics permission to mutate without dissolving identity. The goal is not to chase every new signal. It is to recognize when the old bait has become poison.

A tactic is a lease on behavior, not a title deed.

And the lease is expiring while you read this.

The judge laid down bait. The bait built a movement. Assume your market is at least as clever as an insect, and considerably better organized.

**Cockroach Test**—*What customer, employee, regulator, or citizen behavior must remain static for your strategy to work—and what evidence would prove it has already changed?*

*Assume the target of your strategy is learning from it faster than your dashboard is.*

# Metabolism Before Mythology

. . .

Every business eventually encounters an ancient biological inconvenience:

It must eat.

This was not always obvious during the Unicorn Era. Customers were optional. Margins were a future feature. Cash burn signaled ambition. Product-market fit was defined as the moment immediately preceding the next funding round.

Valuation became nourishment.

Capital became oxygen.

The income statement became fan fiction.

Then rates rose, capital developed questions, and the organism remembered that stories do not metabolize until somebody pays.

## An internal recycling economy

Most cockroaches host an ancient bacterial endosymbiont called *Blattabacterium* inside cells associated with their fat bodies. Cockroaches store nitrogenous waste as uric acid; genomic research indicates that the symbiotic system can reclaim nitrogen from compounds associated with uric-acid degradation and use it in pathways that provision amino acids and other nutrients.[18]

The popular shorthand—"cockroaches turn toxic waste directly into protein"—is too simple.

The more defensible principle is better:

**A resilient organism maintains machinery capable of recovering value from material another organism would discard.**

Silicon Valley would call this closed-loop resource orchestration, appoint a Chief Circularity Officer, and raise $180 million.

The cockroach calls it metabolism.

## Stored optionality

Every organization holds resources whose value is easy to miss during abundance: cash reserves, unused borrowing capacity, historical data, reusable code, supplier goodwill, cross-trained employees, institutional memory, dormant customer relationships, and equipment with spare capacity.

Call the biological metaphor a corporate urocyte if you must, but do not put it on a tote bag.

The optimized company asks, "Why is this not fully utilized?"

The Cockroach Company asks, "Under what future condition does this become food?"

Unused is not automatically valuable. Old code can be technical debt. Empty space can be vanity. Institutional memory can be a polite name for refusing to change. A reserve must have a plausible use under a defined scenario, a known carrying cost, and a credible path to mobilization.

Otherwise it is not optionality.

It is archaeology.

## Metabolism before mythology

Revenue feeds the organism. Gross margin determines how nourishing that revenue is. Cash measures how long the organism can keep searching for food. Debt is stored obligation. Equity is external nourishment purchased by surrendering part of the organism. Valuation is what somebody imagines the organism could become.

Valuation can be useful. It can attract people, finance growth, acquire competitors, build infrastructure, and create liquidity. But valuation cannot pay the electricity bill until somebody converts the story into cash.

Every mania eventually reaches its primitive moment. A railroad must move freight. A bank must collect on loans. A retailer must sell goods for more than the total cost of supplying them. An AI company must answer the question sophistication keeps postponing:

*Who pays whom for what—and why does that remain true after competitors also acquire AI?*

The organism does not care how beautiful the narrative is.

It has a metabolism.

External capital builds metabolism when it purchases capability that can eventually replenish the organism—science, manufacturing, distribution, regulatory capacity, durable cost advantage, a product customers will fund, or recurring cash flow. Otherwise, it merely delays recognition.

It is postponing the autopsy.

---

***Runway is distance from compulsion:***

*The distance between today and the moment another party can force the company to make a decision it knows is strategically stupid.*

---

## The animal that learned to live in our walls

The German cockroach, *Blattella germanica*, did not conquer the modern world by building its own infrastructure.

It conquered ours.

A 2024 study analyzed genome-wide markers from 281 cockroaches across seventeen countries on six continents. The researchers concluded that the species likely evolved from the Asian cockroach about 2,100 years ago through adaptation to human settlements in what is now India or Myanmar, then spread along routes of commerce and human movement. Today it is globally common in human-built structures and essentially absent from natural habitats.[19]

This may be the most offensively elegant startup strategy in natural history.

The German cockroach did not build ships, railroads, warehouses, apartment blocks, restaurants, central heating, or international trade routes.

We did.

It inspected thousands of years of human capital expenditure and reached the obvious conclusion:

*Lovely infrastructure.*

*Shame if somebody monetized the crevices.*

## The economic crevice

The warmest commercial crevices are often the least photogenic: compliance reconciliation, industrial maintenance, payroll, medical coding, logistics exceptions, legacy integration—the load-bearing line items executives complain about but cannot delete.

*Unicorns prefer open savannahs where total addressable markets can be projected to the horizon.*

...projected to the horizon by analysts who have never successfully predicted the weather on a Tuesday. Cockroaches prefer the narrow gap behind the refrigerator, because the refrigerator is already plugged in—where the customer already has a budget, and the problem arrives every Monday.

Before spending a billion dollars to construct an ecosystem, ask whether somebody else has already paid for the warm pipe.

Do you need to build payments, or can you ride existing rails? Do you need a new customer behavior, or can you enter a workflow customers already perform? Must you build distribution, or can you partner with someone who already has it? Do you need an enormous foundation model, or does the customer care only that the domain-specific task gets done?

Own what creates strategic control. Rent what is becoming a commodity. Partner where relationships create leverage. Use commons where commons exist. Preserve portability.

Own the customer problem more deeply than you own the machinery currently solving it.

## Every warm pipe has an owner

Build on someone else's cloud, marketplace, payment rail, model API, social platform, or app store, and you inherit enormous leverage.

You also inherit an owner.

That owner can raise prices, change rules, restrict access, enter your market, alter ranking, comply with a regulation that destroys your economics, or decide you are no longer cute.

Every convenience casts a dependency shadow. Cloud scale can become cloud captivity. An AI API can become model dependence. Venture speed can become a forced-sale clock. A superstar employee can become key-person risk. A giant customer can become a private regulator.

Every superpower eventually sends an invoice.

Ask three questions:

---

*Which dependency can kill us?*

*How quickly?*

*What would substitution cost—in money, time, trust, and degraded service?*

---

## The Winter Food Test

For every apparently underused asset, ask:

What specific winter makes this valuable? How quickly can we mobilize it? Does the option it preserves justify the carrying cost?

If no credible winter turns it into food, throw it away.

---

*Cockroaches are scavengers.*

*They are not archivists.*

---

## The fewer-assumptions company

A five-thousand-year company cannot know its future product, technology, capital structure, geography, ownership, or organizational form. It cannot know whether "employee" will remain the relevant category or whether its next competitor will be a corporation, autonomous software system, cooperative network, open-source community, or legal form not yet invented.

It cannot survive by predicting these things correctly.

It can survive only by reducing the number of predictions upon which survival depends.

That is the Fewer-Assumptions Company. It assumes technologies change, customers learn, capital has seasons, leaders leave, suppliers fail, regulations move, and every moat erodes. It assumes the environment is under no obligation to honor the strategic plan.

Then it does something modern management finds almost indecent.

It responds to reality.

## The Molt

Metabolic discipline can become another form of stupidity. Companies can hoard cash, underinvest in research, preserve obsolete assets, reject useful capital, and become so proud of being bootstrapped that smallness changes from a circumstance into a religion.

*There is no virtue in starving elegantly.*

Metabolic sovereignty is the ability to choose when to consume reserves, raise capital, invest aggressively, compress, scavenge, or build—without having those choices dictated by immediate existential dependence.

**Cockroach Test**—*What apparent waste could become winter food—and what apparent asset is a dependency in expensive clothes?*

*The German cockroach learned to live in our walls.*

*The modern company learned to live in somebody else's cloud, currency, payment rail, shipping lane, grid, and peace treaty.*

*Then it forgot those were dependencies because the invoices arrived on time.*

# The Gods Make Weather

. . .

In 2008, the plumbing of global finance burst through the ceiling.

The banks failed, and the state found money.

The household failed, and the state found a form.

Millions of people learned a lesson—fairly or not—that would outlive the emergency programs: when institutions large enough to threaten the system suffered, government arrived with industrial pumps; when ordinary families flooded, help came with eligibility criteria, telephone music, and a reminder that call volumes were unusually high.

The crisis ended on the calendar.

Its legitimacy aftershock did not.

Then came the long recovery, which looked very different depending on whether a person owned assets, owed rent, billed by the hour, or had access to a central bank through several intermediaries and a tasteful lobby.

The economy healed.

The scar learned politics.

### 2020

The pandemic arrived and exposed the architecture underneath abstraction.

The supply chain turned out to have countries in it.

The cloud required buildings. The delivery app required drivers. The hospital required nurses, oxygen, masks, maintenance, and people willing to stand close to danger while another class of worker discovered that the mute button was a labor-saving technology.

"Essential" became the compliment society gives workers immediately before asking them to absorb a risk the balance sheet would prefer not to recognize.

Companies called the shock unprecedented. Workers called it Tuesday with a virus.

## Geography returns from its sabbatical

War returned energy, shipping lanes, ports, food, fertilizers, chips, transformers, and industrial capacity to the language of national security.

Natural gas rediscovered geopolitics. Oil rediscovered inflation. Semiconductors rediscovered borders. Governments that had spent decades praising frictionless markets began subsidizing factories, screening investment, restricting exports, and explaining that industrial policy was not industrial policy when printed on patriotic stationery.

World military spending reached $2.887 trillion in 2025, the eleventh consecutive annual increase. Civilization was investing heavily in resilience, although it continued to define resilience as the ability to survive what its weapons might do.[20]

The Gods did not disappear.

They changed procurement categories.

## The steering wheel and the axle

By 2026, 68 percent of respondents across OECD countries still believed voting influenced what governments did.

Only 31 percent believed people like them had a say in government decisions. Forty percent reported high or moderately high trust in national government; 43 percent reported low or none.[21]

---

*They believe the steering wheel works.*

*They are less convinced it is connected to their axle.*

---

That gap is not proof of revolution. History is not a vending machine into which one inserts distrust and receives an uprising.

It is evidence of a political-agency deficit: citizens who still participate, still vote, still obey most laws, still pay most taxes—and increasingly suspect that the institutions requesting their compliance have mistaken procedure for consent.

## The young inherit the invoice

Global youth unemployment stood at 12.4 percent. Roughly 260 million young people were outside employment, education, or training.[22]

Those numbers contain radically different lives: young women excluded from paid work, graduates waiting at the edge of professions, migrants, workers trapped in informality, and people whose first experience of adulthood is being told simultaneously that talent is scarce and their labor is surplus.

The credential bargain was never universal. It was nevertheless powerful: study, qualify, work, become secure.

Examination scandals weaken the first verb.

AI unsettles the third.

Housing costs mock the fourth.

Then respectable institutions express surprise when a generation treats respectability as a branding problem.

## War and technology share the calendar

The International Monetary Fund's July 2026 outlook described the global economy as being pulled in opposite directions by two powerful forces: the energy shock from war in the Middle East and a technology-driven investment boom. It projected global growth of 3.0 percent for 2026 and 3.4 percent for 2027, while revising global headline inflation to 4.7 percent for 2026.[23]

Technological summer and economic winter can occupy the same calendar.

AI can become more capable while workers feel less secure. Data-center investment can surge while local grids strain. A nation can gain strategic capacity while a neighborhood receives the exhaust. A company can automate tasks while preserving the approvals that made the tasks slow. A market can create extraordinary wealth while millions experience the future primarily as a higher monthly payment.

That is not contradiction.

It is distribution.

## Who owns the sky

Be precise about what this is not. The dollar still anchors the majority of the world's reserves; American power still ranks first on the serious indexes—at some of the lowest scores those indexes have recorded. This is not collapse. It is *contested primacy*: Rome discovering that several provinces now have semiconductor fabs, sovereign wealth funds, and group chats. Industrial policy stopped being socialism the moment the incumbent adopted it and gave it a different font.

---

*For forty years, the West preached the gospel of frictionless global markets to the rest of the planet. It took exactly one semiconductor shortage for Washington to rediscover the undeniable eroticism of the state subsidy.*

---

Trade did not deglobalize; it fragmented—more of it conducted on exceptional terms, less on normal ones, every exception carrying a flag.[24] The system is not ending. It is being renegotiated, in public, by parties who no longer pretend the old terms were natural.

## The Gods

The Gods in this book are not supernatural beings, and they are not a secret committee meeting beneath a volcano.

They are institutions powerful enough to change other people's weather: states, central banks, courts, militaries, capital markets, hyperscalers, regulators, dominant platforms, elite professional institutions, and corporations so large that an internal decision becomes somebody else's external environment.

They move borders, currencies, tariffs, chips, armies, energy, law, the price of time, the terms of access, and the vocabulary through which suffering becomes legible.

Most people and most companies control none of these things. They live beneath them.

---

*The Gods do not need to hate the cockroach; weather has no opinion of the animal underneath it. But the animal must have an opinion about the weather.*

*That is why the animal needs a survival strategy.*

---

The next four chapters are not a prophecy. They are a stress map.

# PART II

## THE FIVE AI WINTERS

*The next question is not whether AI survives the winter. It is who survives AI.*

> *DISPATCH · INDIA · JUNE 21, 2026. More than two million candidates sit the medical entrance examination again because the first result was voided after a paper-leak scandal. Families pay again—in travel, lost work, coaching, time, and anxiety—for one chance. Outside the test centers, queues form beneath cameras, biometric checks, police, and the old promise: study, qualify, belong.[25] The insult that named this generation came from a courtroom. The arithmetic that radicalized it came from queues like these. Part II is about that arithmetic: how a technology can succeed while the company, worker, investor, community, or institution holding it freezes.*

· · ·

The animal is real. Now the weather changes.

For most of artificial intelligence's modern history, an AI winter meant one familiar sequence. Promises outran performance. Money chased the promises. Disappointment chased the money. Funding retreated, journalists changed adjectives, and researchers who had spent three years being introduced as prophets returned to the less remunerative title of professor.

That history matters. It can also mislead us.

The next AI winter may arrive without the technology becoming stupid. Models may improve. Adoption may spread. Consumers may receive enormous value. Governments may subsidize infrastructure on a scale normally reserved for wars, banks, and other institutions too important to experience ordinary capitalism.

And still, companies may freeze.

They may freeze because intelligence becomes too cheap to defend a margin; because the tool works while the organization refuses to change; because steel, silicon, copper, electricity, transformers, permits, water, or public legitimacy do not arrive on the schedule promised by the data-center brochure; or because capital rediscovers that revenue and expenditure are not merely two colors on a slide but opposing forces with an ancient habit of meeting.

The old winter asked whether AI would work. The new winter asks who captures the value, who carries the cost, who receives permission to operate, and who remains alive when those answers separate.

There is no single AI winter.

There are five weather systems, and the one that matters is the first one capable of killing you.

# The Five AI Winters: AI Can Win While You Freeze

. . .

*AI is going to win.*

*That sentence will bankrupt people.*

It is the intellectual equivalent of standing in 1999 and shouting "The Internet is the future!" while buying Pets.com at a $300 million valuation. The trend was right. The corpse was still dead.

In 2025, private AI investment in the United States reached $285.9 billion. By 2026, 88 percent of surveyed organizations reported using AI in at least one function. Documented AI incidents had risen from 233 to 362 in a year. Yet deployment of AI agents remained in the single digits across nearly every business function.[26]

The technology had colonized the strategy deck faster than it had colonized the operating system.

The phrase *AI wins* smuggles five different promises into one coat: technological success—models become more capable and useful; vendor success—the companies selling them earn durable profits; investor success—capital receives attractive risk-adjusted returns; organizational success—employers convert capability into measurable outcomes; and social success—benefits exceed harms and are distributed tolerably.

These outcomes can travel together. They are not married.

**Technology success ≠ vendor success ≠ investor return ≠ organizational productivity ≠ social value.**

A model can pass the benchmark while the company operating it fails the income statement. A vendor can prosper while customers achieve little. An employer can cut costs while society inherits weaker apprenticeship, greater surveillance, or a new class of people technically employed and economically disposable. Consumers can gain enormous value while investors discover that abundance is magnificent for civilization and inconvenient for margins.

Technology success is the beginning of the economic question. It is not the answer.

## The category dies; the capability goes to work

On 9 May 1973, an audience gathered at London's Royal Institution to watch serious men disagree about AI in public. Sir James Lighthill had reviewed British research and found much of its grander ambition wanting. Donald Michie answered with a film of a machine assembling a model. John McCarthy defended the field. The BBC preserved an impressive machine on a screen, eminent minds on a stage, and no consensus about what the performance meant.[27]

The simplified history fits neatly on a slide: AI overpromised, Lighthill exposed the gap, funding collapsed, winter arrived. The real history was messier—basic versus applied science, institutional rivalry, public funding, and disagreement about what research was for. The report became a symbol of winter, not the snowflake personally responsible for the climate.

The expert-systems boom of the 1980s supplies the more useful precedent. Rule-based systems performed valuable work in diagnosis, configuration, and industrial decision support. They were also brittle outside anticipated conditions, and the knowledge inside them was expensive to extract, encode, update, test, and maintain.[28]

Then the category lost glamour. The capability did not disappear. It migrated into ordinary software, search, configuration tools, decision support, and industrial control.

**The category died. The capability went to work.**

A current AI company should find that prospect more frightening than technical failure. Generative AI may alter civilization, while a generative-AI company becomes as distinctive as a *company with a database*. A technology can triumph so completely that its label loses economic meaning.

I entered technology through Y2K: a real defect amplified into panic, procurement, modernization, and labor-market transformation. The category vanished after midnight. The capabilities, careers, cleaned data, replaced systems, and invoices remained. AI will not be considerate enough to choose only one identity either.[29]

## Five winters, five ways to freeze

By 8:07 on Monday, a founder learns the financing round will take longer than expected.

At 8:19, the largest customer requests a price cut because AI was supposed to reduce delivery cost.

At 9:31, a journalist asks about a data incident.

At 9:42, the model provider announces a new pricing tier.

By ten, the company has experienced all five winters before the catered hummus develops a skin.

**Capital Winter** begins when money becomes scarcer, slower, more expensive, or merely curious enough to ask a second question. It does not require aggregate AI investment to collapse. Category-level summer does not make company-level payroll. A nation can pour hundreds of billions into AI while one vendor discovers that the round is delayed, the lender has repriced risk, the customer will not prepay, and salaries remain stubbornly attached to the calendar. The Gods upstream may include a central bank, sovereign technology policy, pension allocations, export controls, or geopolitical uncertainty. The founder experiences the result as a personal verdict delivered by someone in a fleece vest. Often it is weather wearing a name badge. The fatal mechanism is time. Salaries, cloud commitments, leases, debt covenants, and customer obligations arrive on schedule. Financing does not. The fragile response is emergency capital followed by indiscriminate cutting. The Cockroach response is reversible commitments, customer-funded learning, credible unit economics, and enough metabolic independence to reject money that rewrites the organism.

**Margin Winter** begins when capability spreads faster than pricing power. Models improve. Open alternatives mature. Interfaces standardize. States subsidize domestic capability. Hyperscalers bundle the feature into software the customer already buys. The miraculous differentiator becomes an API call, then a checkbox, then a sentence the salesperson has been asked to remove because the customer assumes it is included. The technology succeeds. The rent does not. The fragile response is to add features, rename the bundle a platform, and hope vocabulary can defend gross margin. The Cockroach response is to move differentiation outward—to proprietary context, workflow, distribution, accountability, regulatory capability, physical execution, and relationships that do not reproduce when model weights are downloaded. Margin Winter shortens the capital clock. The shortened clock forces the layoff. The layoff fires the reviewer. The missing reviewer causes the data leak. The leak triggers the Legitimacy Winter. You didn't die of five separate diseases; you died of a cascade.

**Productivity Winter** begins when the tool works but the organization does not change. A model drafts the memo in thirty seconds. The memo still waits nine days for approval. An agent recognizes the customer's problem; policy forbids the remedy. A coding assistant produces a patch; undocumented architecture makes review slower than authorship. The company purchases intelligence at the edge while authority remains at the center, then expresses surprise that the edge has become an expensive waiting room. Technology is purchased because procurement can buy an object. The complements—decision rights, incentives, training, data quality, process ownership, exception handling, liability, and trust—are political. The fragile response is another pilot. The Cockroach response is to redesign the work and measure outcomes rather than licenses.

**Infrastructure Winter** begins when the cloud remembers that it is steel, silicon, copper, concrete, land, water, electricity, transformers, permits, networks, debt—and neighbors. A data center may be commissioned in a few years. A grid connection, turbine supply chain, transmission line, or public settlement may require longer than the founder's vesting schedule. Infrastructure Winter does not require the world to run out of electricity. It requires one company to need one resource before that resource exists—or before the community agrees to provide it. The fragile response is to assume somebody else's balance sheet will absorb the constraint, or to lock in long commitments at the top of the cycle. The Cockroach response is workload efficiency, portability, explicit substitution plans, and a degraded mode that remains useful when preferred infrastructure is unavailable or unaffordable.

**Legitimacy Winter** begins when the system loses permission to operate. The permission may be legal, contractual, professional, social, or political. It disappears when customers no longer trust data practices, regulators reject voluntary assurances, employees discover that *human in the loop* means a human hidden behind the curtain, creators reject uncompensated extraction, or communities are asked to accept pollution and public subsidy as the price of somebody else's valuation. The rise in documented incidents does not prove every deployed system became less safe; deployment volume and reporting practices matter. It does show that the surface on which a technical error can become an institutional crisis is expanding.[26] The fragile response is public relations supported by a legal memo. The Cockroach response is traceability, incident readiness, meaningful oversight, customer exit, data rights, clear liability, and ethical boundaries that harden under pressure instead of melting on contact with revenue.

*Count what the five winters just repossessed: the available capital, the defensible moat, the scarce intelligence, the hospitable infrastructure, the political tolerance. Those are the clauses of the Unicorn Company's operating wager—the one the Prologue said was not absurd item by item, only fatal taken together. Part II is that design flaw, itemized by season.*

| Winter | Fatal misdiagnosis | Cockroach response |
| --- | --- | --- |
| Capital | Raise emergency money and cut indiscriminately. | Build reversible commitments and autonomous metabolism. |
| Margin | Subsidize a price the market no longer accepts. | Own scarce layers above the model. |

| | | |
|---|---|---|
| Productivity | Buy a more capable tool. | Redesign work, authority, and incentives. |
| Infrastructure | Lock in capacity or hope. | Improve efficiency, portability, and degraded mode. |
| Legitimacy | Change the disclaimer font. | Build auditability, accountability, and permission. |

A company can survive the original weather and die from the cure.

*A bridge round is often just a payday loan wearing a fleece vest.*

## How weather enters the body

The Gods change the environment. The Winter is the economic transmission mechanism. The Six Cs are the organs where the damage will eventually appear. The Molt is the change made before damage becomes death.

Energy shock → Infrastructure and Capital Winter → Compute and Cash → route workloads, reduce commitments, preserve degraded mode.

Model commoditization → Margin Winter → Customers and Cash → move value toward workflow, context, trust, and accountability.

Labor controversy → Productivity and Legitimacy Winter → Capabilities and Culture → redesign work, apprenticeship, oversight, and distribution.

The point is not to paint thirty boxes. The point is to locate the first place where weather becomes an organ failure—and install a fire door before the smoke arrives.

*A company can survive the weather and die from the cure*

**UNICORN AUTOPSY · BUILDER.AI**—Builder.ai promised to make app development as easy as ordering pizza through an AI-enabled platform called Natasha, supported by human engineering teams. It attracted prominent investors and entered insolvency in May 2025. The Financial Times reported that provisional internal figures revised estimated 2024 revenue from $220 million to roughly $55 million and raised questions about potentially bogus or uncollectible sales. Lenders declared default. These were reported findings during an unfolding insolvency and investigation, not final judicial determinations of every disputed fact.[30] Several winters stacked. Debt and investor financing had become load-bearing. Confidence in the financial and technological narrative collapsed. Human-intensive delivery sat uneasily beneath the promise of automated creation. Increasingly capable coding tools made an expensive intermediary harder to defend. Builder.ai did not fail because AI stopped improving. It failed while AI was improving rapidly.

*Verdict: Narratively brilliant. Metabolically impossible.*

## The countercase: attach AI to an institution

Thomson Reuters is not a model wearing a hoodie. It owns legal, tax, accounting, compliance, and professional-information products embedded in high-consequence workflows.

For full-year 2025, the company reported 7 percent organic revenue growth overall and 9 percent across its three principal professional segments. In the first quarter of 2026, organic revenue rose 8 percent overall and 9 percent across those segments. Those figures do not isolate AI's causal contribution. They do reveal a different metabolism.[31]

Customers pay not merely for a clever answer, but for authoritative content, recurring workflow, distribution, institutional trust, and an organization prepared to stand behind high-stakes outcomes.

Builder.ai attached an AI narrative to delivery.

Thomson Reuters is attempting to attach AI to an institution.

**Incumbency buys time to adapt. It does not buy the adaptation.**

## Winters stack

A Margin Winter begins with a customer asking for a discount. The discount shortens the capital clock. Cost cuts remove reviewers and customer knowledge. Errors rise. Renewals pause. Fundraising makes bad news impolite. The founder centralizes every exception. What entered as a pricing problem leaves as a legitimacy crisis.

Add Infrastructure Winter: the provider reprices, a cloud region constrains capacity, data rights narrow, or power arrives late. The company may be robust to each event alone and fragile to their correlation.

Capital plus Legitimacy collapses trust exactly when remediation becomes expensive. Margin plus Infrastructure creates a vice: customers demand lower prices while compute commitments remain high. Productivity plus Capital strands organizational redesign before the complements mature. Legitimacy plus Command turns every incident into a centralized panic because nobody near the problem is authorized to act.

The company does not need a theatrical probability for every combination. It needs to know whether one shock propagates into the others.

Designing survival around six simultaneous sunny days is not strategy.

It is prayer with a quarterly review.

## The Molt

The Five Winters are a diagnostic, not a horoscope. Preparedness can become hoarding, premature austerity, or a new priesthood selling bronze insects and maturity certificates.

The framework earns its keep only when it changes a decision before the weather changes it for you.

The question is not whether AI wins. It is who survives the winter you are already in.

> **Cockroach Test**—*Which of the Five AI Winters can kill your organization first—and which second Winter would the first one drag through the door?*

---

*AI can win while you freeze.*

---

# The Winter of Abundance

. . .

In November 2022, querying a model performing around GPT-3.5 level on a widely used benchmark cost roughly twenty dollars per million tokens.

By October 2024, comparable performance cost about seven cents.

A decline of more than 280-fold in roughly eighteen months.[32]

It is the sort of number that makes investors smile until somebody explains what falling prices do to suppliers.

Technology culture is trained to fear scarcity: not enough chips, models, data, talent, or compute. The more subversive possibility is abundance. AI may succeed so thoroughly that intelligence becomes cheap, widely accessible, and increasingly substitutable—and that success will destroy the economics of companies whose only moat is access to intelligence.

The winter arrives not because the brain stops working.

It arrives because everybody can rent one.

## The state and the meter

The state may want intelligence cheap for the same reason an industrial power wants electricity cheap. The vendor may want it scarce for the same reason the utility enjoys the meter.

National strategy and company margin can point in opposite directions.

By 2026, Stanford's AI Index described the performance gap between leading American and Chinese models as effectively closed, with models from the two countries trading the lead since early 2025. The United States still produced more top-tier models and attracted far more measured private investment; China's government guidance funds and industrial deployment complicated any comparison based only on venture dollars.[26]

The strategic point is not that one country has already won. Scarcity can be attacked deliberately. States can subsidize compute, open tooling, chips, training, power, procurement, and deployment because diffuse cheap capability may strengthen the national system even while it weakens the margin of any one vendor.

A company built on permanent scarcity can therefore lose to technological progress, platform bundling, open models, or industrial policy—then hold a conference about the democratization of AI while quietly revising guidance.

## From miracle to utility

Electricity created enormous industries and productivity gains, yet using electricity stopped being a differentiated strategy. Value migrated into motors, appliances, factories, networks, processes, and organizational redesign. Electricity remained indispensable while becoming strategically ordinary.

AI may follow the same path. At first, access is scarce, and the model appears magical. Then performance spreads, interfaces standardize, prices fall, alternatives improve, and the customer asks the impolite question:

*What have you built above the intelligence?*

Model capability may remain powerful, expensive at the frontier, and strategically important. But the defensible layers increasingly move outward:

| Layer | What remains scarce as model access spreads |
|---|---|
| Proprietary context | What a generic model does not know about the customer, domain, or history. |
| Workflow | Where intelligence enters action, and exceptions are resolved. |
| Distribution | The right to appear where the user already works. |
| Trust | Confidence accumulated through reliable performance. |
| Accountability | An institution willing to explain, correct, and bear liability. |
| Physical execution | The ability to move atoms, deliver care, repair machinery, or operate infrastructure. |
| Institutional legitimacy | Permission to act inside a profession, jurisdiction, and community. |

The farther value moves from the raw model, the harder it is to reproduce by downloading another one.

## DeepSeek and the price of surprise

DeepSeek became a case study in bargaining power before it became a stable pricing philosophy.

In February 2025, the company announced additional open-source releases and steep off-peak API discounts. Later price changes moved in both directions. Whatever mixture of commercial, scientific, and national strategy produced the sequence, the durable fact was simpler: a credible alternative changed expectations, bargaining power, and the cost curve.[33]

The lesson is not to *use DeepSeek*. Prices, models, suppliers, export rules, and capacity change. The lesson is not to build immortality on one provider's current scarcity—or current generosity.

Every API price is a strategic fact with an expiration date.

## The countercase: GitHub Copilot

Commoditization does not make every AI product a low-margin wrapper. GitHub Copilot shows how abundance can strengthen a product when intelligence is embedded inside workflow and distribution.

Microsoft reported rapid growth in GitHub Copilot adoption during 2025 while GitHub expanded model choice inside the same developer environment.[34]

User count is less important than architecture. GitHub need not depend on one exclusive model. Its value can rise as models proliferate because it owns repositories, identity, collaboration, governance, pull requests, security, and the place where generated code becomes organizational software.

The moat moved from the brain to the environment in which the brain becomes useful.

If you do not own the environment, you are a tenant in somebody else's building.

*And the landlord can change the locks.*

## Accountability is a product

A generic model can suggest a tax position. A professional institution must decide whether it is defensible, document the basis, and remain present when an auditor objects.

A model can identify an anomaly in a medical image. A healthcare system must determine whether it changes treatment, who sees the result, who may override it, and who answers when the result is wrong.

A model can draft a contract. An institution must know which jurisdiction governs it, which clause transfers risk, whether the source material was privileged, and who will still be reachable when the counterparty discovers the machine's confidence was decorative.

Liability-bearing is not merely overhead.

It is part of the product.

*Accountability is not overhead. It is the product. Startups cannot manufacture fifty years of legitimacy with a better prompt.*

*In an abundance economy, the answer becomes cheap.*
*The promise to answer for the answer does not.*

## AI may automate the rent before the job

Suppose AI lowers the cost of a service by 20 percent. The seller imagines margin expansion. The buyer asks why the price has not fallen 25 percent.

Competition decides which instinct survives.

When rivals adopt comparable tools, efficiency can dissipate through lower prices, higher expectations, or intensified service. The technology may automate part of the economic rent before it eliminates the entire occupation.

A durable firm uses cheap intelligence to deepen what remains scarce: context, relationships, guarantees, exception handling, physical execution, and permission to operate.

Every technology begins as a noun and matures into infrastructure. The adjective *AI-powered* will eventually be buried beside *interactive, cyber, cloud-based,* and *blockchain-enabled*—each of which once justified a markup and now describes a toaster.

The toaster is interactive. The toaster is in the cloud. The toaster is AI-powered. It still burns the toast, and no one applauds because the funeral for the adjective has already occurred.

## Cheaper per task, larger in total

The final inversion is Jevons with GPUs.

The International Energy Agency reported that energy use per AI task had been falling by at least an order of magnitude annually in recent years—an efficiency improvement it described as unprecedented in energy history. Yet global data-center electricity demand rose 17 percent in 2025, and electricity use in AI-focused data centers rose 50 percent. More efficient simple queries were joined by reasoning, video, and agentic workloads that can consume hundreds or thousands of times more energy per task.[35]

Efficiency did not shrink the appetite.

It enlarged the menu.

Cheap intelligence can therefore destroy unit economics and expand the market at the same time. Falling unit prices can coexist with rising revenue, higher aggregate spending, and greater physical demand. Frontier research remains capital-intensive. Models are not perfectly substitutable. The future will not become one free beige slurry merely because a benchmark converged.

But the direction of the test is unforgiving.

If your business strengthens as models improve and cheapen, you are building above the commodity.

If it requires intelligence to remain scarce, expensive, and exclusive, you are shorting technological progress while marketing yourself as its champion.

---

*When an AI hallucinates a tax fraud, you cannot put an algorithm in federal prison. The premium of the future is the human being legally authorized to take the blame.*

---

## The Molt

Abundance is not universal access. Cheap API tokens do not erase scarce chips, unequal electricity, language gaps, data rights, or the institutions that decide who may act on an answer.

But scarcity is no longer entitled to remain your business model merely because it once appeared on the investor deck.

> **Cockroach Test**—*If your preferred model became free tomorrow, what would customers still pay you for? Write the answer in one sentence. If it contains the word "model," start over.*

---

*The intelligence is becoming a utility.*

*The bill for pretending otherwise is addressed to your org chart.*

---

# The Productivity Winter: Who Gets the Productivity?

. . .

The missing technology is the organization.

At 9:00, a manager pastes a forty-page document into an AI assistant.

At 9:01, the screen produces a summary, risk list, draft email, and table of actions.

At 9:02, someone asks who is authorized to act.

Legal needs to review the risks. Compliance must approve the summary. Procurement says the pilot license cannot be used in production. Data Governance has concerns about the source document. The executive sponsor leaves for another meeting titled *Accelerating AI at Scale.*

Three months later, the company has purchased four thousand licenses, launched six pilots, held an offsite, and changed no process.

I have spent three decades in rooms like this.

The technology changes.

The ritual remains stubbornly interoperable.

## There is no bottom line. There is a frontier.

The empirical record is not contradictory.

It is conditional.

In a controlled experiment involving 453 college-educated professionals, Shakked Noy and Whitney Zhang found that access to ChatGPT reduced completion time for writing tasks by roughly 40 percent and improved evaluated quality by about 18 percent.[36]

In a preregistered experiment with 758 consultants, AI users completed 12.2 percent more tasks and worked 25.1 percent faster on tasks inside the model's capability frontier. On a complex task deliberately placed outside that frontier, users with AI were 19 percentage points *less* likely to reach the correct answer.[37]

Then the evidence moves from tasks to institutions. S&P Global found that the average organization scrapped 46 percent of AI proof-of-concept projects before production, while the share abandoning most of its initiatives rose from 17 percent to 42 percent.[38]

Put those results on one slide and an executive will demand the bottom line.

There is no bottom line.

There is a frontier.

AI helps when the task is well represented, context is available, output is easy to evaluate, supervision is competent, and the cost of error is bounded. It helps less—or harms—when tacit context is deep, quality is difficult to judge, the workflow cannot absorb the output, or the user cannot detect when confidence has outrun competence.

The question is not *does AI work?*

It is: *For whom, on which task, inside what system, under whose supervision, with what consequence?*

## Tutor or treadmill

A study of 5,172 customer-support agents found that AI assistance increased issues resolved per hour by 15 percent on average, with the largest gains among less experienced and lower-skilled workers. Some of the gains persisted when the system was temporarily unavailable, suggesting the assistant had transmitted practices from stronger workers to newer ones.[39]

That is the optimistic architecture: compressed apprenticeship. Expert patterns arrive in the moment of work rather than being entombed in a knowledge portal where documents go to become immortal and unread.

The same system can become a treadmill.

If a novice becomes productive faster, does management invest the gain in training and higher-value work—or hire fewer novices? If the model performs the easy tasks through which judgment was once developed, who becomes tomorrow's expert? If the organization captures the practices of its strongest employees, who owns the resulting knowledge, and what bargaining power remains with the people who produced it?

Technology can be a tutor or a treadmill.

Organizational design decides which.

## The most expensive work begins after the impressive output

AI can generate code. The developer must determine whether the code belongs. AI can draft a contract. The lawyer must locate the liability. AI can generate a forecast. The manager must decide what action the forecast justifies. AI can summarize a complaint. Someone must still possess the authority, budget, and judgment to solve it.

Work is a chain, not a collection of isolated tasks. Accelerating one link can merely create a faster queue at the next.

That is why evidence from experienced software developers matters. In an early-2025 randomized study, METR found that developers working in familiar open-source repositories took 19 percent *longer* with AI tools. By early 2026, METR believed newer tools were probably helping more, but selection effects and unreliable time measurement prevented a trustworthy new estimate.[41]

That is not an argument that AI makes developers slower. It is an argument against replacing workflow diagnosis with a screenshot of the model completing a toy task.

A brilliant model inserted into a stupid sequence does not produce a brilliant organization.

It produces the same queue with better prose.

## Who gets the productivity?

Suppose AI saves a team ten thousand hours.

The spreadsheet records an opportunity.

The institution decides what the hours become: lower prices. Higher margins. Shorter days. More customers. Better quality. Fewer employees. More ambitious work. Training. Or ten thousand additional hours of meetings about capturing the opportunity.

"Hours saved" is not an outcome.

It is a distribution decision waiting to happen.

The machine does not decide who receives the gain. Ownership, competition, bargaining power, regulation, leadership, and culture decide. Productivity is therefore not merely a technical property. It is a political outcome inside the firm.

A company can use AI to create a shorter workweek, expand service, deepen quality, lower price, widen access, or improve resilience. It can also convert every gain into a headcount target while preserving every approval layer that made the work slow.

Calling the second choice *technology strategy* does not make it less of a choice.

It merely gives the choice a dashboard.

IBM offers a useful ledger. The company says AskHR handled more than 11.5 million interactions and one million transactions in 2024 while its HR operating budget fell 40 percent over four years. In 2025, CEO Arvind Krishna said AI had replaced the work of several hundred HR employees even as total employment rose through hiring in software engineering, sales, and marketing.[42]

That is not a simple layoffs parable. It is a distribution decision: routine work disappeared, investment moved, and the institution chose where the released capacity went. The question is not only how many jobs vanish. It is whether saved capacity becomes stronger capability—or merely a smaller payroll.

## The ladder with the first rung removed

Stanford's 2026 AI Index reported that employment among American software developers ages twenty-two to twenty-five had fallen nearly 20 percent from 2024, while employment among older developers continued to grow. The Index did not establish AI as the sole cause; hiring cycles, interest rates, post-pandemic correction, and other forces matter.[43]

The fact still belongs in this chapter.

AI is not entitled to claim every missing job. Skeptics are not entitled to ignore a contraction concentrated at the entrance to an exposed occupation.

Management keeps asking whether AI can perform the junior analyst's work.

The more important question is how the senior analyst becomes senior after the junior work disappears.

We spent decades calling entry-level labor inefficient and are now surprised that civilization had hidden apprenticeship inside it.

The junior task is often repetitive because the novice is learning the terrain: where the data lies, which customer detail matters, why the exception exists, when a confident answer should be distrusted, and how institutions behave when the rule meets a human being.

Delete that path and the organization may save salary today while quietly liquidating tomorrow's judgment.

The cockroach identity that entered this book emerged from examination failures, unemployment, and a generation doubting whether credentials still purchased a legitimate entrance into institutional life. That identity is Indian. The threatened bargain is not.

A society can survive a technology that eliminates tasks.

It becomes less stable when it eliminates the credible path by which young people become useful, independent adults.

## A profession that automates its larvae

By mid-2025, McKinsey's technology leadership said that more than three-quarters of roughly 43,000 employees used its internal generative-AI platform, Lilli, monthly. Reporting described the system assisting with research, proposals, and slide drafting—work traditionally assigned in part to junior staff. McKinsey argued that automation did not necessarily imply fewer junior analysts.[44]

The important question is not whether one consultancy will reduce a particular intake class. It is architectural:

A profession that automates its larvae must explain how it intends to produce adults. The two hundred and sixty million young people standing in exam queues in Delhi, Manila, and London are not just a labor statistic. They are the larvae we are burning to keep the quarterly margins warm.

---

*You cannot incubate a fifty-year-old partner with "judgment" if you starved them when they were a twenty-two-year-old analyst. You are eating your own seed corn and calling it margin expansion.*

---

We spent three decades telling young people to "learn to code" and "become knowledge workers." The moment they did, we handed the knowledge work to a server farm in Memphis and told them to learn to weld. You are turning your firm into an hourglass: heavy at the top with aging partners, heavy at the bottom with AI agents, with a completely hollow middle that will eventually snap under its own weight.

Every profession has an apprenticeship metabolism. Medicine has supervised practice. Law has research, drafting, and review. Engineering has testing, debugging, and maintenance. Consulting has analysis, interviews, models, and slides. Accounting has reconciliations, exceptions, and close cycles.

The repetitive work is not all sacred. Much of it deserves automation. But when the easy work disappears, learning must become more deliberate, not merely less expensive.

A Cockroach Company does not preserve obsolete junior tasks for nostalgia. It preserves the path to judgment: supervised novice work; rotations through exceptions and incidents; human review that explains rather than merely approves; time for experts to teach; and promotion based on judgment acquired, not volume of routine output. Apprenticeship is infrastructure. Budget it accordingly.

## The Productivity J-Curve—and its favorite alibi

During the ERP era, I watched companies buy systems whose process models assumed clean data, clear ownership, standard work, and disciplined governance.[45]

The software arrived.

The assumptions did not.

Management either forced a bad process into the new system and called it transformation, or customized the new system until it reproduced every historical dysfunction at enormous cost. AI projects are repeating the pattern at higher speed: agents before exceptions are documented, copilots before decisions are redesigned, intelligence at the edge while authority remains at the center.

Economists Erik Brynjolfsson, Daniel Rock, and Chad Syverson describe a Productivity J-Curve around general-purpose technologies. Organizations must invest in complementary intangible capital—processes, skills, business models, and redesign—before measured gains fully appear.[46]

This is hopeful.

It is also the favorite alibi of every failed transformation.

Every program that produces no result can claim to be heroically waiting on the left side of the J.

The Cockroach Company requires evidence that work is changing: cycle time, resolution, error, customer outcome, rework, learning speed, risk, approval latency, or the number of people newly authorized to act.

A six-month field experiment across 66 firms and 7,137 knowledge workers found that integrated generative AI reduced time spent on email and after-hours work but did not detect broader changes in task quantity or composition.[40] The tool created real individual relief. The organization did not automatically reorganize itself around the relief.

A pilot that changes neither a decision right, a workflow, a job description, an approval matrix, nor an outcome measure is a demonstration.

A demonstration is not transformation merely because the catering was excellent.

## The Molt

Productivity Winter can become a refuge for incumbents. Workflow complexity and risk are real constraints; they are also familiar excuses for protecting hierarchy from tools that make hierarchy less necessary.

The answer is not to wait for certainty. It is to experiment quickly, measure real outcomes, redesign authority, protect apprenticeship, and demand learning after action.

> **Cockroach Test**—*Which process in your organization would remain slow, political, or stupid even if the model became infinitely intelligent?*

---

*Name, out loud, in a meeting with the door open, who gets the hours.*

---

# Every Cloud Has a Flag, a Power Bill, and a Capital Structure

. . .

From the banks of the Mississippi, the cloud has a substation.

In South Memphis, the former Electrolux site became home to xAI's Colossus supercomputer. In May 2025, the Greater Memphis Chamber announced that Phase I had connected to a newly constructed substation supplying 150 megawatts from Memphis Light, Gas and Water and the Tennessee Valley Authority, with another 150 megawatts of battery storage intended to ride through outages and demand-response events.[47]

The numbers sound digital only until one remembers what a megawatt is.

Then the story becomes local: transmission, generation, permits, construction, jobs, taxes, air quality, grid capacity, and neighborhood trust.

The future of AI arrives in a city not as a glowing brain but as industrial infrastructure with neighbors.

The cloud is somebody else's building, grid connection, cooling system, supply chain, permit, financing package, jurisdiction—and political dependency.

There is no cloud.

There is land with branding.

There is no cloud without land, law, power, and jurisdiction.

There is a flag over every substation.

## The global percentage and the local grid

The International Energy Agency estimated that data centers consumed about 485 terawatt-hours of electricity in 2025 and projected roughly 950 terawatt-hours by 2030—about 3 percent of global electricity demand. Global data-center consumption rose 17 percent in 2025; AI-focused facilities grew much faster.[48]

Three percent sounds manageable until it lands in one place.

Nearly half of American data-center capacity is concentrated in five regional clusters. Data centers can be built in two or three years; generation, transmission, interconnections, turbines, transformers, and permitting often move more slowly. Shortages in high-bandwidth memory, advanced chips, transformers, and grid capacity can constrain projects before the model encounters its first user.

Infrastructure Winter does not require the world to run out of electricity.

It requires one company to need one resource before that resource exists.

The cloud sounds weightless.

The agent waits for a transformer.

*The cloud isn't in the sky. It is a concrete box in Memphis drinking a river to generate a picture of a cat. And that river has local voters.*

Silicon Valley sold us a post-physical utopia. It turns out the utopia requires the energy consumption of Argentina, a copper mine in Chile, and a zoning variance from a highly irritated city council in Tennessee. You cannot "disrupt" your way out of a zoning hearing.

## Memphis: the promise and the invoice

The Memphis case contains both columns of the infrastructure bargain.

Regional advocates describe major investment, construction work, technical employment, grid upgrades, visibility, and the beginnings of an AI cluster. A 150-megawatt substation and matching battery system are real industrial capability, not a pitch-deck adjective.

The project also generated environmental and legal conflict.

In April 2026, the NAACP and its Mississippi State Conference sued xAI and an affiliate under the Clean Air Act, alleging that dozens of gas turbines serving the Colossus 2 project had operated without required permits. In May, the plaintiffs sought a preliminary injunction. In June, the U.S. Department of Justice moved to intervene and dismiss, arguing that Mississippi had determined no permit was required for the challenged equipment. The parties disputed the law, operating status, turbine counts, emissions, and jurisdiction; the case remained pending as this manuscript closed.[49]

That qualification belongs in the body because litigation is not a metaphor and an allegation is not a verdict.

So does the structural lesson.

Speed can create competitive advantage while colliding with environmental law, public process, public health, and local trust. The investor sees a campus. The utility sees a load. The regulator sees a source. The resident experiences the air, noise, traffic, rates, jobs, and whether anyone asked.

Legitimacy is part of infrastructure.

A substation can be built in months.

Trust, once destroyed, has a longer interconnection queue.

## Constraint is a design discipline

Infrastructure is not only a ceiling. It can force better architecture.

Smaller models, quantization, caching, batching, task routing, efficient chips, and flexible workloads reduce the need to feed frontier compute to routine work. A company that sends classification, extraction, translation, drafting, and simple support through the same premium model has a simple architecture.

So does the invoice.

A resilient design uses deterministic software for deterministic tasks, smaller models for routine language work, frontier systems where the frontier matters, and humans where consequence remains high.

The cloud provider may call this complexity.

The cockroach calls it not feeding caviar to the stapler.

## Compute Sovereignty

Sovereignty is not independence. An organism with no dependencies is called dead.

Compute sovereignty is the capacity to choose among dependencies before one becomes sovereign over you.

It requires four disciplines:

| Discipline | Operating question |
|---|---|
| Economic visibility | Do we know the full cost of inference, storage, networking, monitoring, evaluation, human review, failure, and urgency? |
| Architectural portability | Can the customer problem survive a change in model, region, chip, or provider? |
| Graceful degradation | What useful service remains when preferred compute is unavailable, restricted, or repriced? |
| Political and physical literacy | Where does the infrastructure sit, how is it powered, which laws and export rules govern it, and who bears its effects? |

Cloud efficiency can become captivity. A model API can become a private regulator. Data residency can become a product requirement overnight.

## The physical dependency has a financial twin

According to the IEA, capital expenditure by five large technology companies exceeded $400 billion in 2025 and was expected to rise another 75 percent in 2026—more than projected global investment in oil and gas production. The buildout had become too large to be financed by corporate balance sheets alone; capital markets were increasingly load-bearing.[48]

The question is no longer whether AI infrastructure is expensive.

It is who carries the demand risk if revenue arrives later than the concrete.

Investor scenarios have framed the buildout as a $600 billion, $840 billion, or roughly trillion-dollar revenue question. These were arguments about demand risk—not audited holes in the economy or prophecies carved into marble.[50]

The skeptic says *bubble* and imagines the analysis complete.

The promoter says *infrastructure* and makes the same mistake.

## The bonfire and the railway

The telecom boom around the turn of the millennium offers the canonical case. Companies laid fiber, leased routes, financed networks, and projected explosive demand. Firms failed, and assets were repriced. Much of the physical network nevertheless became substrate for cloud computing, streaming, e-commerce, and broadband.[51]

Some overinvestment was theater. Some was rational provision for lumpy, fast-growing demand. Some firms built useful assets with fatal capital structures.

The fiber did not need the original shareholder to survive.

*Firm value can go to zero. Infrastructure value can persist.*
*Salvage value depends on repurposing cost and who buys at the bottom.*
*Financing liability remains with whoever signed.*

The railway may outlive the railway promoter. The question is who financed the bridge—and who was standing underneath it when the capitalization fell.

But GPUs are not fiber. Semiconductors depreciate quickly. Steel lasts differently from silicon; transmission differently from models; customer trust differently from all three.

A railway metaphor cannot rescue every purchase order.

The post-boom scavenging belongs later. For now, the lesson is narrower: useful infrastructure and sound investment are related questions, not synonyms.

If the AI boom ended tomorrow, which assets, skills, customer relationships, and infrastructure would still be valuable after the story burned away? That list is your railway. Everything else on the balance sheet is bonfire.

## They are all looking at the same cloud

The state sees strategic capacity. The hyperscaler sees utilization. The investor sees return. The startup sees an API. The utility sees load. The regulator sees a source. The community sees a power plant.

They are all looking at the same cloud.

## The institutions that taught us to worship the weather

The Five AI Winters have separated the climate from the creature.

Capital can freeze while aggregate investment remains abundant. Margins can freeze because technology succeeds. Productivity can freeze inside organizations that bought intelligence but preserved stupidity. Infrastructure can freeze beneath a cloud with land, law, and neighbors. Legitimacy can freeze when speed outruns permission.

These winters are not acts of nature. Institutions amplify them—through the ways we finance companies, educate managers, reward spectacle, outsource judgment, and convert uncertainty into PowerPoint certainty.

The next Part enters the temple.

*The cockroach has survived the weather. Now it must survive the priesthood.*

# PART III

## EXCOMMUNICATING THE ELITES

> *DISPATCH · NEW DELHI · JULY 21, 2026. The roses came back to Jantar Mantar, and this time the state answered with water cannon and tear gas; police counted nearly one hundred eighty injured by nightfall. Four days later the education minister resigned. The elites this Part prosecutes did not gas anyone. They practice a politer extraction—legible, billable, and slide-ready. But the crowd and the boardroom are reading the same ledger of who pays for whose mistakes, and the injured are counted by the police.*[2]

· · ·

The problem is not that elites are stupid.

Many are brilliant. That is what makes the error expensive.

The Five AI Winters are not acts of nature. Institutions amplify the weather. Financiers turn the price of a protected security into a diagnosis of enterprise health. Accelerators turn a five-minute pitch into a mating display. Business schools provide the protagonist, the exhibits, the decision point, and—most luxuriously—the assurance that an answer exists. Consultants convert judgment into a rented service and consequence into passive voice. Executives celebrate innovation while dismissing the people who know why the old machine makes that noise.

The indictment is precise: every institution selects for a local form of fitness and eventually begins to mistake that test for reality itself.

A funding round selects for investor persuasion. Demo Day selects for compressed narrative. A management case selects for reasoning from curated evidence. A consultancy selects for problems that can be framed, staffed, analyzed, and concluded inside an engagement. A quarterly dashboard selects for outcomes visible before the next reporting date. These are real capabilities. They are not the same capability as surviving winter.

# The Horn Is Glued On: Valuation, Demo Day, and Fundability Fitness

. . .

You met the animal in the Prologue—the ordinary horse with an implausible object protruding from its forehead, notarized at a billion dollars. That was the description. This chapter is the accusation.

---

*The horn is not merely mythical. It is attached. The adhesive has a term sheet.*

---

An entire generation was told to spend its twenties chasing the animal without ever being shown the tube of glue.

The conference room is designed to make skepticism feel underdressed: floor-to-ceiling glass, sparkling water shaped like laboratory equipment, and a founder in black sneakers announcing that the company has become a unicorn. Applause follows. One billion dollars is the sort of number that makes adults clap even when nobody can explain exactly what has been priced, which rights came with the security, or whether the customer has been informed that mythology now appears on the balance sheet.

The slide shows a horse with a horn. Nobody asks to see the adhesive.

## The rights are legal. The headline is mythology.

A private-company valuation is commonly reported like a medical diagnosis: the company is worth one billion, ten billion, forty-seven billion dollars. The sentence sounds complete. It is not. In a financing round, an investor buys a particular class of shares under a particular contract—and that contract is not paperwork. It is a private constitution.

Liquidation preferences, seniority, anti-dilution protection, vetoes, redemption rights, and return guarantees do not merely divide money. They allocate power over the company's future. They also distinguish the investor's protected security from the common stock held by founders and employees.

The headline valuation usually multiplies the price of the newest preferred share by the fully diluted share count, as though every share carried the economics of the most protected one. If an investor buys $100 million of preferred stock at a reported $1 billion post-money valuation and the company later sells for $500 million, the proceeds do not obey the press release. They obey the contract. The announcement describes one company. The cap table contains several economic species occupying the same legal body.

Will Gornall and Ilya Strebulaev examined the disclosed contractual terms of 135 U.S. venture-backed companies reported to be worth more than $1 billion. Their model estimated reported post-money valuations at an average of 48 percent above fair value; 65 of the 135 fell below the billion-dollar threshold after contractual protections were incorporated; common shares were estimated to be overvalued by an average of 56 percent.[52]

These are model estimates, not tablets delivered from Mount GAAP. The durable principle is less theatrical: the price paid for the most protected share is not the value of every share—or the health of the enterprise beneath it.

The rights are legally binding. The hallucination is the headline.

---

*The founders get the Forbes cover, the investors get the liquidation preference, and the employees get common-stock lottery tickets to a drawing that was canceled last Tuesday.*

---

A billion-dollar valuation is just a socially acceptable form of corporate cosplay until the Series D wire actually clears. The entire Silicon Valley compensation model is basically feudalism with a ping-pong table.

## When a transaction becomes a species

The investor pays a price for a protected security. A database multiplies that price across the capitalization. Journalism reprints the database. The founder inserts the journalism into the next deck. Recruiters repeat the headline to employees whose options carry none of the investor's protections. By lunch, a financing term has become a biological classification, and the myth has leased office space.

Once the company is called a unicorn, ordinary evidence passes through the glow. Rapid hiring becomes proof of demand. Losses become investment. Founder eccentricity becomes vision. A large office becomes culture. The animal is assumed healthy because the horn is expensive.

---

*Valuation is where the operating wager becomes identity—and an identity, unlike a wager, does not get re-underwritten every round.*

---

WeWork supplied the public dissection. Its 2019 registration statement reported approximately $1.82 billion of 2018 revenue, a net loss of approximately $1.61 billion, extensive lease obligations, related-party transactions, and governance arrangements that public investors could finally read in one place. The planned offering was withdrawn weeks later. The company was real. The private headline had simply priced a different animal from the one the filing described.[53]

## The countercase: the price of possibility

A high valuation is not automatically body paint. Moderna reached public markets with no approved product, years of scientific uncertainty, substantial accumulated losses, and a pipeline whose future customers could not finance the work in advance. Its 2018 financing and IPO purchased experiments, clinical programs, manufacturing capability, regulatory work, and time. Years later, that platform helped produce a COVID-19 vaccine at extraordinary speed.[54]

That outcome does not sanctify every valuation. It establishes the boundary condition: current revenue can dramatically understate scientific options, intellectual property, or infrastructure that customers cannot fund before it exists. The question is not simply whether the company is profitable today. It is whether capital is creating independent capability—or financing a larger version of an unresolved dependency.

## Then the animal learns to perform

Once the horn is attached, the company enters another habitat: Demo Day. The stage has a time limit, visual grammar, professional audience, and compressed decision. In that environment, certain traits become adaptive—a large market, a clean category, a memorable founder story, confident projections, prestigious credentials, and a future vast enough to make present economics look provincial.

These traits are not meaningless. Founders must communicate; investors need filters; early-stage companies lack years of operating evidence. But every selection system breeds what it can see. A five-minute pitch cannot directly observe maintenance quality, succession depth, moral courage, customer necessity, or the ability to survive eighteen bad months. It evaluates proxies. Some are intelligent. Some are demographic. All are partial.

Demo Day selects for what can be judged quickly. Customers select for what remains useful after the applause.

Dana Kanze and colleagues found that men were more often asked promotion-focused questions about upside while women were more often asked prevention-focused questions about risk. The different questions elicited different answers and correlated with different funding outcomes.[55]

Ask one founder, "How large can this become?" Ask another, "How will you prevent churn?" The first is invited to narrate possibility; the second must defend against failure. Investors then compare the excitement of the answers and conclude that one founder possesses more vision. The bias need not announce itself. It arrives disguised as diligence.

The repair costs nothing: ask every founder both questions, and grade the answers rather than the framing.

Generative AI makes polish cheaper still. Market maps, competitive quadrants, biographies, financial models, and decks can now be manufactured at industrial scale. When the appearance of preparation becomes abundant, serious selection must move deeper: customer references, retention, technical diligence, evidence of judgment under contradiction, and proof that the team can change its mind when reality earns the right.

## Perfect for the room; unwanted in the wild

Quibi entered the market in April 2020 with Jeffrey Katzenberg, Meg Whitman, Hollywood relationships, approximately $1.75 billion in financing, and a clean thesis: premium short-form video for mobile viewing. Six months later, it announced that it would shut down. The market wanted video. It did not want enough Quibi. Investors selected it in conference rooms; consumers selected it in the wild. Its leaders then closed, returned remaining capital, and sold assets rather than converting error into a zombie.[56]

Investor selection can create real value. Ventures just above angel-funding thresholds later showed better survival and operating outcomes than closely comparable unfunded firms.[57]

Capital, certification, networks, and narrative matter. The test is partial. A company that spends every week optimizing the pitch may eventually become a pitch with payroll.

## The Molt

None of this indicts ambition, storytelling, or the billion-dollar outcome that occasionally deserves the number. It indicts a habitat that breeds for its own test—and a company that begins mistaking success inside that habitat for evidence of health everywhere else.

---

*Every habitat breeds for what it can measure.*

*The danger begins when it calls that measurement fitness.*

---

# Venture Capital Is Weather, Not Entrepreneurship

. . .

Venture capital did not merely finance entrepreneurship. It colonized the noun.

In 2001, Ben Chestnut and Dan Kurzius built an email tool because clients of their Atlanta web-design business needed one. There was no dorm-room mythology and no investor announcing that email was a trillion-dollar category hiding in plain sight. Mailchimp grew without outside equity until Intuit acquired it in 2021 for total consideration of $12 billion.[58]

Business media repeatedly called Mailchimp a "bootstrapped unicorn," as though a successful enterprise required retroactive admission into the zoological category it had avoided. Revenue had funded the company for two decades, but the language still needed venture capital to validate the species.

A 2026 working paper assembled data on more than 100,000 professionals affiliated with U.S. venture firms. Among investors with recorded investments, fewer than 40 percent were ever credited with a successful investment, while 5 percent generated roughly 90 percent of investment profits.[59]

The result describes a concentrated system. It does not tell you that the individual across the table is incompetent. It does tell you that proximity to a successful institution is not the same thing as demonstrated investment skill.

Many people wearing the vest are not Midas. Some are standing near him in a group photograph.

---

*...and they have learned to point. They didn't invent the future; they rode a fifteen-year wave of artificially suppressed interest rates and mistook a macroeconomic subsidy for personal genius.*

---

If you lower the cost of capital to zero, people will inevitably fund a Bluetooth-enabled juicer. That is not innovation. That is just what happens when money is so cheap it loses its will to live. It is the only industry on earth that treats making a profit as a quaint, slightly embarrassing lifestyle choice.

## One financing product ate the dictionary

Entrepreneurship is the creation of an enterprise under uncertainty. Venture capital is a financing technology designed for a subset of those enterprises: high uncertainty, scalable economics, large possible outcomes, and a plausible path to liquidity sufficient to compensate for many failures.

The distinction should be obvious. Yet *startup* came to imply a ritual: raise, hire, burn, scale, raise again, exit. A founder financing growth through customers is "bootstrapped," as though revenue were an emergency improvisation involving footwear. A durable regional firm employing hundreds remains a "small business." An unprofitable software company becomes "high growth" after purchasing customers with subsidies.

The vocabulary ranks identities, then guides talent, media, policy, and university attention toward the most visible financing events. Firms asking for less capital become less legible precisely because they ask for less.

Venture capital is a financing technology. Entrepreneurship is the discipline of creating value under uncertainty.

## The portfolio and the body

Venture portfolios are governed by power-law outcomes: a few extraordinary winners drive fund returns. In a survey of 885 institutional venture capitalists, investors considered the management team somewhat more important than the product and viewed deal selection as their most important source of value. Under early-stage uncertainty, that is rational. It also means human beings are being evaluated through incomplete evidence, networks, pattern recognition, status, and judgment—not by an oracle.[60]

The Kauffman Foundation reached a similar conclusion from the limited-partner side: hope had weakened due diligence inside the institution charged with performing it.[61]

The fund is a portfolio. The company is a body.

The fund can rationally support many uncertain experiments because one enormous outcome may compensate for several complete failures. The founder lives in only one experiment—with payroll, customer promises, employee careers, years of work, and usually the largest concentration of the founder's financial and emotional capital.

---

*The investor sleeps on a portfolio. The founder does not sleep at all.*

---

## The cap table is also a calendar

The clocks diverge. A conventional fund has an investment period, reserves, a harvesting phase, and an expected life. A founder may wish to compound a useful company for thirty years. The investor may need liquidity within ten. Neither intention is immoral. The conflict begins when the clocks remain unspoken until a strategically sound next decade collides with a financially necessary next transaction.

Money is never just money. Debt asks for scheduled payment. Customer revenue asks for value now. Family capital may ask for patience or control. Public equity asks for disclosure and a continuously repriced story. Venture equity asks for an outcome large and liquid enough to matter to a portfolio. Every dollar writes a clause into the organization's constitution.

And the clauses have authors upstream of the person across the table. The venture capitalist is not God. The venture capitalist has limited partners. The limited partner has liabilities. The pension fund has beneficiaries. The sovereign fund has a state. The interest rate has a central bank. By the time the founder is told "the market has changed," several Gods have already touched the weather.

---

*The founder experiences "VC appetite" as a personal evaluation. Much of it is climate.*

---

## Capital–Organism Fit

The mature question is not "How much can we raise?" It is "What future action will this money make difficult to refuse?" A biotechnology platform with years of pre-revenue research should not be financed like a consulting practice capable of invoicing in month one. A semiconductor manufacturer cannot fund a fabrication plant through annual subscriptions and positive thoughts. A model wrapper should not automatically consume $100 million merely because another company's science requires it.

Saras Sarasvathy's effectuation research supplies the strategic complement. When the future cannot be forecast reliably, entrepreneurs often begin with means already controlled, build stakeholder commitments, exploit contingencies, and limit exposure through affordable loss rather than maximizing hypothetical return.[62]

Affordable loss is not timidity. It is preserving the ability to play again after the forecast misbehaves.

Capital that buys learning, infrastructure, science, manufacturing, distribution, or strategic independence is nourishment. Capital that merely postpones business-model truth is anesthesia. Mailchimp's customer-funded history shows what a different clock can permit: time to serve a fragmented market, compound in a crevice, and preserve the option to sell later rather than requiring a sale to remain alive.

Here, once, is the full defense the book owes the financiers. Biotechnology, semiconductors, energy, aerospace, and advanced manufacturing contain long gestation periods and irreducible costs. Future customers cannot prepay for every molecule, fabrication process, or propulsion system that may fail. Organized early-stage finance creates enterprises that would not otherwise exist.

The weather sometimes waters the crops. The error is building a species that dies whenever it stops raining.

## The Molt

Bootstrapping has its own priesthood. It can starve research, delay hiring, underpay people, and turn founder control into a substitute for governance. Customer revenue can hijack a roadmap; debt is inexpensive until revenue contracts. The doctrine is anti-dependency, not anti-capital: choose a capital clock compatible with the organism you are trying to build.

---

*Venture capital is weather. Entrepreneurship is the animal. Take the rain when it helps. Never let the meteorologist rename the species.*

---

# The Priesthood of Legible Extraction

. . .

Singapore, 2006. A marble-floored boardroom overlooked Marina Bay. The presentation ran to roughly three hundred slides. The proposal involved moving approximately eleven thousand manufacturing jobs to Shenzhen. The labor-arbitrage logic was polished. Big Four partners were present. Every head in the room nodded, including mine.[67]

## Four seconds

Three hundred slides.

Eleven thousand jobs.

Transfer cost, milestones, labor savings, implementation risk—all modeled, all defensible, all nodding.

Then a junior analyst asked:

*"What happens when they don't need us anymore?"*

Four seconds passed.

Somebody changed the slide.

---

*PowerPoint does not make people evil.*
*It just formats the evil into bullet points so nobody has to look it in the eye.*

---

. . .

Months later, in the account I subsequently published, the transferred operation surpassed the original facility's peak performance at substantially lower cost. The closing message from China was colder than the severance calculation: the new operation no longer required the original team's technical support. It had learned what we knew and improved upon it.[67]

We had modeled the transaction. The analyst had asked about the organism. Every credentialed, brilliant, expensively educated head in the room chose, in four seconds, not to know.

---

*My hands still remember that silence. My résumé does not mention it.*

---

The spreadsheet was not wrong.

It was incomplete in exactly the direction our incentives preferred.

That silence is the subject of this chapter. Not evil. Not stupidity. A machinery built from four ordinary parts, each defensible alone: abstraction, legibility, incentives, and outsourced judgment.

Abstraction converts people into categories so decisions can scale. Legibility keeps what can be framed, counted, and presented. Incentives attach money and fear to the count. Outsourced judgment ensures that by the time the consequence arrives, the person who recommended it is three engagements away.

Business schools teach what can be framed. Metrics reward what can be counted. Consultants sell what can be packaged. The danger is not intelligence. It is intelligence operating at a distance from consequence.

Watch the language do the killing so no one has to. "Four thousand people will lose their jobs" becomes "a workforce-efficiency opportunity has been identified." Notice there is no longer anyone in the sentence.

---

*An opportunity was identified by no one, affecting four thousand nobodies, and it rolls down a waterfall chart into a bucket labeled synergies.*

---

Nobody has lied, exactly. Responsibility has been converted into a slide transition. PowerPoint does not make people evil. It formats the evil into bullet points so nobody has to look it in the eye—moral distance made visually elegant, and billable.

A 300-slide deck is not an analysis. It is an anesthetic. It is explicitly designed to numb the executive team's conscience just long enough for them to sign the severance checks. In the Middle Ages, the priesthood offered absolution for sins in exchange for gold. Today, consulting firms offer absolution for layoffs in exchange for equity. The liturgy changed; the racket remained intact.

Begin with the seminary. The business-school case is a remarkable instrument: a protagonist, a problem, curated facts, numbered exhibits, and a room in which consequential decisions can be rehearsed without injuring actual employees. It also contains a luxury reality never provides: somebody has decided what belongs in the case, and the ending already exists.

Operators receive no such amenities. At 2:13 a.m., the customer is leaving, the model provider has changed terms, the data are incomplete, and the person with the relevant memory retired as a "legacy resource." There is no Exhibit 14. The answer may not exist; the problem itself may be misidentified.

Rakesh Khurana's history of American business schools traces an unfinished attempt to make management a profession with broad obligations, followed by a drift toward technical expertise, market-centered models, and credentialing. The drift did not make the education useless. It changed the default questions—which investment has the highest return, which incentive aligns the agent, which unit destroys value—and a question need not be wrong to become dangerous. It merely needs to become the only question in the room.[63]

Daron Acemoglu, Alex He, and Daniel le Maire studied appointments of business-degree managers in U.S. and Danish firms and reported that, within five years, wages and labor share declined in the settings studied without corresponding measured gains in output, investment, or employment growth.[64]

The result is provocative, not universal. It nevertheless asks an indecent question: what if modern management education has become unusually good at teaching managers how to redistribute value while allowing them to experience the redistribution as value creation?

Sumantra Ghoshal warned where that can lead: theories built on narrow assumptions about self-interest may normalize the practices they claim merely to describe.[65]

Treat employees as agents to be controlled, and they become inventive at gaming the controls. Apply enough pesticide, and you do not eliminate adaptation. You select for pesticide-resistant behavior.

Wells Fargo manufactured the proof at industrial scale. In 2016, the Consumer Financial Protection Bureau fined the bank $100 million over the widespread illegal practice of opening unauthorized accounts. The bank's contemporaneous analysis identified more than two million potentially unauthorized accounts; the CFPB pointed to sales targets and compensation incentives as drivers.[66]

The scandal becomes organizationally convenient when narrated as a story of unethical employees. Thousands of people did not independently awaken with the same creative idea. The system defined success, attached reward and fear to the measure, and made missing the target personally dangerous. Management then expressed astonishment that the organization produced the number rather than the purpose beneath it.

A metric is not a window. Once money and authority attach to it, it becomes a selection pressure.

Before compensation attaches to any number, somebody should have to ask what a clever, frightened, ambitious person could do to maximize it while damaging the purpose underneath. That question should be required before graduation. It is not on the syllabus.

Then there is my own guild. Consultants solve real problems: pattern recognition, temporary capacity, specialized knowledge, independence from internal politics. A board facing a merger, cyber crisis, or complex implementation may be irrational not to seek outside expertise. The danger begins when expertise becomes a substitute nervous system.

An organization lacks a capability. Advisers analyze the problem and build the answer. The client implements it without acquiring the ability to generate, challenge, maintain, or modify the reasoning. The next adjacent problem appears, and the client needs the advisers again—not because the first engagement failed, but because it succeeded without changing who could think.

The OECD has documented the mechanism in public institutions: external providers can supply scarce skills and accelerate delivery, but over-reliance can hollow out the knowledge needed to define needs, hold suppliers accountable, and adapt systems over time.[68]

A sophisticated procurement department can lower the day rate and completely miss the price of not knowing. The client still legally owns the system. Practically, it cannot explain why the system works, challenge a change request, or operate after the external team leaves.

And when the distance grows long enough, it acquires a legal docket. In December 2024, the U.S. Department of Justice announced a $650 million criminal-and-civil resolution involving McKinsey's work for opioid manufacturers, including a 2013 engagement advising Purdue Pharma on steps to "turbocharge" OxyContin sales. McKinsey's U.S. subsidiary entered a five-year deferred-prosecution agreement covering obstruction and misbranding-related charges.[69]

A former senior partner later pleaded guilty to destroying records with the intent to obstruct the investigation. In May 2025, he was sentenced to six months in federal prison, two years of supervised release, 1,000 hours of community service, and a $40,000 fine.[70]

Nothing in the client-service machinery required the human consequence to remain visible. That is the indictment.

The prosecution owes the defense a coda. Management knowledge, honestly transferred, creates real value. A randomized experiment in large Indian textile firms found that intensive process consulting raised productivity by 17 percent in the first year—through repeated observation and changed routines, not PowerPoint as moral perfume.[71]

Toyota's Production System Support Center operates with the same architecture as capability transfer. In one post-Katrina partnership, Toyota reported that average home-rebuild time fell from 116 days to 60, with the explicit aim that the people doing the work could continue after Toyota left.[72]

A useful engagement has two deliverables: the immediate result and the client's increased ability to operate after the outsiders leave. The second is harder to display in the closing presentation and occasionally inconvenient to the adviser's future pipeline. It is nevertheless the difference between intervention and dependence.

Buy expertise. Borrow perspective. Rent temporary capacity. Never rent your judgment without an exit plan.

Here is the strangest fact of 2026. The Edelman Trust Barometer found business trusted by 64 percent globally, eleven points above government, and rated more ethical and competent than every other institution.[73]

Do not celebrate. Interrogate. The last trusted institution is the one conducting the restructurings, deploying the AI, and writing the euphemisms. Business is not trusted because it earned absolution. It is trusted because everything else fell further—which means it is holding, on borrowed time, an asset this chapter has watched the priesthood convert into slideware.

---

*The junior analyst was the only person in the Singapore room practicing management.*
*The rest of us were practicing legibility.*

---

# Maintenance Is the Moat

. . .

Knight Capital did not lose more than $460 million because its algorithm became sentient.

It lost the money because one server missed an update and ninety-seven warnings became email.

At the U.S. market open on August 1, 2012, Knight's automated router sent more than four million erroneous orders while attempting to fill only 212 customer orders. The firm traded more than 397 million shares and lost more than $460 million in approximately forty-five minutes. New code had reached seven servers but not an eighth, leaving an obsolete function executable. An internal system generated ninety-seven emails identifying an error, but the messages were not formal alerts, and nobody acted in time.[74]

Four hundred and sixty million dollars in forty-five minutes. Maintenance had finally produced a visible metric.

## The work whose success looks like nothing

Innovation receives a launch. Maintenance receives a ticket. The launch has executives, lighting, branded lanyards, a man in a vest saying *journey,* and a sentence about changing the world.

Call her Denise. Every company has one. Denise knows the certificate expires Thursday and has been emailing everyone since March. Nobody reads Denise's email because Denise's email is not a journey. Then Thursday comes, money leaves the building, and everyone wants to know why nobody warned them.

**Denise warned them. Ninety-seven times. But Denise doesn't wear a Patagonia vest, so nobody listened.**

---

*We build statues to the arsonists who invent the fire,*

*But we minimum-wage the people holding the fire extinguishers.*

---

The "innovator" breaks things and moves fast. Denise sweeps up the glass, bandages the bleeding, and begs AWS not to cut the server. Denise is the only thing standing between your corporate database and a teenager in North Macedonia with a ransomware script. Pay Denise. Respect Denise. Build a shrine to Denise.

When innovation works, something happens. When maintenance works, nothing happens. The market does not malfunction. The plane does not cancel. The close does not fail. The data do not leak. The backup restores.

"Nothing happened" is one of the most valuable outcomes an organization can produce—and one of the hardest to reward because the counterfactual remains invisible. Lee Vinsel and Andrew Russell call this cultural bias the innovation delusion: novelty receives prestige while maintenance, repair, care, and institutional continuity are treated as background labor.[75]

This is a class system, and it should be named as one.

Innovation gets the keynote. Maintenance gets the pager.

Innovation announces a future. Maintenance prevents Tuesday from becoming history.

The people who know why nothing happened are precisely the people efficiency programs remove first, because their success leaves no visible output. The maintainer is the cockroach of the org chart: unglamorous, load-bearing, and noticed only when management turns on the kitchen light and discovers how much invisible work was keeping the building operational. That is not an insult. In this book, it is the highest available rank.

For much of my career, I worked inside enterprise performance-management systems. To an executive, the quarter-end close can look like a button. Underneath sit mappings, ownership rules, intercompany eliminations, currency translations, controls, exceptions, and people who remember why one entity's sign convention is reversed. The more seamless the output, the easier it becomes to believe the seam never existed.[76]

A successful close makes the maintenance team look idle. Then the team is reduced, the next close fails, and institutional memory returns as emergency consulting spend.

This is the maintainer's paradox:

---

*Competence erases the evidence used to justify competence.*

---

Maintenance therefore includes more than patches. It includes documentation, succession, training, backups, vendor relationships, data quality, control testing, process ownership, and preservation of the reasoning behind exceptions. A maintained system is not one that never changes. It is one that can change without forgetting why it works.

## Southwest and the cost of neglected recovery

During the 2022 Christmas travel period, Southwest Airlines canceled 16,900 flights and affected more than two million passengers. The U.S. Department of Transportation later imposed a $140 million civil penalty and secured more than $600 million in refunds and reimbursements. Weather initiated disruption across the industry; Southwest's systems and operating model amplified it.[77]

Once crews and aircraft were displaced, recovery became combinatorial; local failures stopped remaining local. The airline possessed aircraft, pilots, demand, and brand. In the critical interval, it lacked the recovery capability to turn those assets back into a schedule.

The later response provides the countercase inside the failure. In December 2025, DOT credited Southwest's $112.4 million investment in its Network Operations Control and improved operational performance, allowing an $11 million portion of the penalty to be satisfied through resilience investment rather than another Treasury payment.[78]

The point is that maintenance can be architecture, staffing, training, command, and capital allocation—not merely a facilities expense. The meltdown made resilience expensive enough to see. It had been valuable before the cancellations.

## Organizations that cannot learn by crashing

Research on high-reliability organizations—aircraft carriers, nuclear plants, air-traffic control—found not perfection but a culture: preoccupation with weak signals, respected redundancy, deference to frontline expertise during anomalies, and social permission to say *something looks wrong* before it becomes a press conference.[79]

Ordinary companies improve by trial and error because another trial usually exists. High-consequence systems face harsher arithmetic: the next error may delete the opportunity to learn from it. In those environments, maintenance is not the department after innovation. It is the condition under which innovation is allowed to continue.

AI intensifies the obligation because the system can change without a conventional code release. Data distributions move. Vendors update models. Prompts change. Attackers learn. New users create failure modes absent from the pilot. NIST's AI Risk Management Framework treats responsibility as a lifecycle—govern, map, measure, manage—rather than a certificate applied once at launch.[80]

AI maintenance therefore means continuous evaluation against real conditions, version traceability, incident review, human escalation, and authority to downgrade or stop a system when evidence contradicts the launch story.

The junior work being automated today is where tomorrow's maintainers learn the exceptions, compromises, failure signatures, and noises nobody documented.

---

*The AI that replaced the junior cannot maintain the system it generates—it only generates.*

*In ten years, when the system breaks, the senior engineer who learned the terrain as a junior will not exist to fix it.*

---

The AI era will require more maintainers precisely as executives are being promised fewer employees. A civilization that deletes its apprenticeships and then deletes its maintenance budget has scheduled its own Knight Capital. Somebody still has to watch the machine. Somebody has to have been taught to watch it. Denise did not arrive fully formed.

## Maintenance as moat

Innovation diffuses. Features are copied. Models converge. Maintenance compounds differently. A company that has spent years understanding a regulated workflow, preserving data quality, documenting exceptions, training customers, patching integrations, and recovering from incidents owns something difficult to reproduce in a weekend hackathon.

The moat may not be the new feature. It may be the accumulated credibility that the feature will still work on Monday. In healthcare, finance, industrial systems, logistics, aerospace, and enterprise accounting, customers do not merely buy capability. They buy continuity, support, liability-bearing, and the promise that somebody will answer when the elegant abstraction encounters Tuesday.

It is the org chart's version of the promise to answer for the answer.

## The Molt

Maintenance can become embalming. Every obsolete system has defenders who call it mission-critical, and every dying product has one customer whose contract renews automatically. Maintenance preserves useful function while enabling renewal. Embalming preserves form after purpose has left. The maintainer must be empowered to say "repair this"—and sometimes "bury it."

Give the maintainers the keynote for one year. Just one. See what fails to happen.

> **MEMO FROM THE OFFICE OF TRANSFORMATION · SUBJECT: NOTHING HAPPENED SUCCESSFULLY**—Leadership is pleased to report that during the reporting period, no systems failed. No customers noticed anything. No regulators called. No data leaked. No executives were interviewed on television against their will. The quarter closed on the day the calendar suggested. Following a comprehensive review of these results, and given the absence of measurable incidents attributable to the Maintenance function, the Maintenance function has been classified as non-value-adding, effective immediately. Affected staff are invited to a webinar titled "Owning Your Journey." The Office of Transformation thanks Maintenance for its years of invisible service and looks forward to discovering, in approximately eleven months, precisely what it was.

# Stop Fighting Like an Empire

. . .

*Valuation is a price, not a pulse. Venture capital is weather, not entrepreneurship. Demo Day is a habitat, not the market. Management education is a lens, not reality. Consulting is leverage, not an external nervous system.*
*Innovation is an option, not an exemption from upkeep.*

Be precise about the enemy, because precision is what lets this Part be savage without becoming cheap.

The enemy is not the venture capitalist. It is dependency mistaken for strategy.

The enemy is not the MBA. It is legibility mistaken for reality.

The enemy is not the consultant. It is borrowed judgment mistaken for capability.

The enemy is not scale. It is scale that requires permanent favorable weather.

The enemy is not AI. It is the assumption that technical capability automatically becomes economic value, organizational productivity, or social legitimacy.

These institutions are staffed by extraordinarily capable people. Their tragedy is structural: every institution eventually mistakes the fitness it selects for the definition of fitness itself.

*The priesthood taught the startup to admire empires: the largest market, the widest footprint, the most expensive adjective, the system so exquisite that failure becomes unaffordable. Power is photogenic. Avoiding a stupid battle is not.*

# The Unicorn Autopsy (Redacted)

. . .

OFFICE OF THE CORPORATE MEDICAL EXAMINER

`POSTMORTEM REPORT · CASE NO. [redacted]-4471 · RELEASED UNDER PROTEST`

*The decedent and all persons named herein are fictional. Any resemblance to your portfolio is a coincidence you should sit with.*

**DECEDENT:** *Synergia Labs, Inc.* ("Synergia"), a Delaware unicorn, age six. Last seen alive at a valuation of $1.4 billion. Discovered unresponsive by a Series D associate performing routine diligence, who attempted revival with a bridge round and, when that failed, a press release.

**EXTERNAL EXAMINATION:** Decedent presents as a standard-issue mythical ungulate in good superficial condition. Coat glossy; recently rebranded, third occurrence. Horn detached on contact. The attachment site shows adhesive residue consistent with a Series C term sheet, applied in layers, most recently over the auditor's objections. Hooves show no wear consistent with contact with the ground.

**INTERNAL EXAMINATION:** Extensive narrative tissue throughout. Cap table presents as several economic species occupying one legal body, in varying states of preference; common stock found at the bottom, flattened. A thorough search of the thoracic cavity located the total addressable market ($4 trillion, laminated) but no customers. A note reading "GTM motion—Q3" was recovered from where the revenue should have been.

**STOMACH CONTENTS:** Fourteen agile coaches, partially digested. Eighty million dollars in unexercised cloud credits. One Chief Purpose Officer, intact, still presenting. Three rebrands. A framework of unknown origin. Traces of a pivot, consumed shortly before death.

**TOXICOLOGY:** Adjective levels several times the survivable threshold: "AI-powered," "category-defining," "full-stack." Burn rate elevated. Runway: not detected.

**CAUSE OF DEATH:** Metabolic asphyxiation. The decedent forgot it needed to eat.

**MANNER OF DEATH:** Ruled a "strategic wind-down" at the family's request.

**CONTRIBUTING CONDITIONS:** Chronic dependence on external nourishment; congenital absence of degraded mode; miracle budget in excess of seven.

**SURVIVED BY:** The founders, who have announced a new venture in an adjacent space and wish the community well. Also survived by four hundred employees, who were paid in the hallucination, and who have not announced anything.

**RECOMMENDATIONS OF THE EXAMINER:** [redacted]. `The Examiner further notes that this is the fourth such decedent this quarter presenting with identical adhesive, and respectfully suggests that somebody inspect the` [redacted] `glue factory.`

Nothing was learned.

. . .

Part IV teaches the opposite anatomy: how the small survive the large on purpose.

---

*Bring the horn if you like.*
*We will use it as a coat hook.*

---

# PART IV

## THE ASYMMETRIC ARSENAL

. . .

The cockroach has survived the priesthood.

Now it must learn not to fight like one.

The priesthood taught the startup to admire empires. The pitch deck points toward the largest market. The strategy retreat asks how to defeat the category leader. The board rewards the widest footprint, the fastest advance, and the most expensive adjective. Power is photogenic. Avoiding a stupid contest is not.

History keeps returning to an impolite fact: the weaker side rarely wins by imitating the stronger side's preferred form of strength. A small firm that attacks a hyperscaler on compute, bundling, distribution, and capital is not necessarily courageous. It may simply be volunteering to convert the incumbent's advantages into weapons.

This Part borrows from military history and doctrine, so the moral boundary is drawn here, once, before the first metaphor leaves the barracks. War is organized violence. A dead soldier is not a failed experiment; a destroyed city is not a pivot; people and communities are not attritable assets. Business may borrow the logic of asymmetry. It may not borrow the romance of suffering.

The first asymmetric advantage is refusing to perform strength in the form the incumbent prefers.

The four chapters that follow are therefore not a theory of conquest. They are a discipline for unequal power: choose terrain that makes scale expensive; make intent clear enough for local knowledge to act; keep uncertain bets small enough to kill honestly; protect the pantry that makes every strategy executable; and separate a failed narrative from a useful capability.

---

*The cockroach does not become a smaller elephant.*

*It learns where the elephant cannot economically go.*

---

# Choose the Terrain; Distribute the Fight

. . .

Rome's answer to Hannibal was not greater theatrical courage. It was refusing to give him the battle he wanted.

In 217 BCE, after Hannibal crossed the Alps and humiliated Roman armies, Quintus Fabius Maximus followed at a distance, occupied favorable ground, harassed supply, and avoided the decisive engagement Roman honor demanded. Plutarch's account is a later moral biography, not a field dispatch, but the strategic shape is clear: Hannibal could win battles. He could not manufacture endless supplies, replacements, local legitimacy, or time.[81]

Romans mocked Fabius as Cunctator—the Delayer—until reality completed the performance review. The lesson is not "move slowly." Speed has no meaning until direction, terrain, and the cost of being wrong are specified. Strategy begins before the contest: choose the terrain on which the incumbent's strength becomes expensive.

## Choose terrain where scale must pay rent

A giant technology company possesses capital, distribution, infrastructure, installed customers, legal teams, brand recognition, data, and the ability to bundle a new feature into software the customer already buys. These are formidable advantages—in a contest where those advantages matter.

So do not select that contest. If the incumbent wins through standardized scale, choose work that resists standardization. If it wins through low-touch volume, choose a problem where trust, liability, and exception handling matter. If it wins through a general platform, choose the workflow the platform regards as administrative mud. If it wins through global reach, choose a regulated or relationship-dense market where arrival is not legitimacy. Marine Corps doctrine distinguishes absolute strength from relative advantage: power matters through its relationship to the objective, the environment, and the opponent's weakness.[82]

The business translation is less majestic. Do not challenge the elephant to a weightlifting contest. Live where weight becomes an inconvenience.

The best crevice is not merely neglected. Neglect can vanish after one earnings call. It is structurally awkward: entering it would require the incumbent to change sales economics, service intensity, risk appetite, or the standardized architecture that makes the larger business efficient.

Choose terrain where the incumbent must become less like itself to follow you.

The asymmetric advantage is not smallness. It is forcing size to pay rent.

---

*When you fight a giant, do not bring a sword.*

*Bring a clipboard, a compliance audit, and a very narrow hallway.*

---

**You do not fight an empire by imitating its supply chain—you fight it by making its scale an administrative burden. Win by being too legally annoying to crush.**

If Amazon wants to fight you in an open field, drag them into a swamp, hand them a compliance audit, and charge them for the mosquito repellent.

### Shopify walks onto Amazon's terrain

Shopify's original elegance was not that it tried to become Amazon. It sold tools to merchants who did not want Amazon to become them. Then Shopify moved deeper into logistics, acquiring Deliverr in 2022 for approximately $1.97 billion. Logistics was strategically relevant—fulfillment shaped the customer experience, and Amazon had trained buyers to expect extraordinary speed. It was also a different anatomy: warehouses, carrier density, inventory, returns, peak capacity, and boxes apparently designed by a malicious geometry department.

In 2023, Shopify sold most of its logistics businesses to Flexport and later reported a net impairment of approximately $1.34 billion associated with those sales.[83]

The figures do not prove the ambition was foolish. They reveal the invoice attached to changing terrain. Shopify entered a contest in which Amazon's decades of physical density mattered enormously. The strategically important act was not only the expansion. It was the retreat. An impairment is painful. An unending tribute to a mistaken battlefield is worse.

I have sat in strategy rooms where the first question was, "How do we beat the leader?" Once the rival was named, the meeting acquired a war map. Features became weapons, hiring became mobilization, and every difference from the incumbent looked like deficiency. Nobody had yet established whether the incumbent's market definition deserved imitation.[84]

The better question is colder: what must the incumbent spend, reorganize, or risk to neutralize one dollar of our effort? If the answer is less than a dollar, we selected terrain that amplifies its strength. If the answer is ten dollars, a custom service model, a new liability structure, or injury to a profitable installed base, our apparent weakness has become leverage. The point is not to boast about being small. It is to make the other side's scale arrive with an invoice.

### Distribute truth, not merely teams

Once the contest moves into a crevice, local reality becomes more important, and headquarters becomes farther away. The organization must distribute action without distributing confusion.

At 11:27 p.m. UTC on January 31, 2017, a GitLab engineer intended to remove data from a secondary database and ran the command on the primary one. Around 300 gigabytes disappeared. GitLab then discovered that multiple backup or replication methods were incomplete, unreliable, misconfigured, or not operating as assumed. The company restored from an older staging backup, lost recent changes, published live notes, anonymized the engineer as "team-member-1," and issued a detailed postmortem.[85]

Transparency did not restore the data. It made the error available to the whole organism. The lesson is not that distributed teams make fewer mistakes. It is that a distributed organization must make intent, operating knowledge, failure, and correction transmissible. Distributed truth, not merely distributed teams.

### Make the center clearer

Mission command is often reduced to empowerment, as though military doctrine were an unusually expensive motivational poster. It is not "everybody do whatever feels authentic." That is Burning Man. Army doctrine is more demanding: competence, trust, shared understanding, commander's intent, disciplined initiative, and prudent risk allow local actors to respond when communication is disrupted and reality changes faster than headquarters can prescribe.[86]

The paradox is the doctrine's heart: the freer the edge must become, the clearer the center must become. Modern corporations often do the opposite. They centralize approval and decentralize ambiguity. The chief executive announces an "AI-enabled future," while operating teams are left to infer the customer promise, legal boundary, data owner, accountability for failure, and budget. Every decision climbs upward because intent never traveled downward.

Mission command centralizes purpose, ethical limits, capital boundaries, and survival constraints. It decentralizes reversible decisions closest to the customer, code, machine, or problem. The center controls the why and what must never be violated. It does not choreograph every leg.

John Boyd's OODA loop—Observe, Orient, Decide, Act—is usually sold as a speed trick. Boyd's deeper concern was orientation: the models, experience, culture, and feedback through which observations acquire meaning. Speed without orientation merely allows the organization to be wrong earlier in the day.[87]

## Watch a fact die of altitude

Hierarchy does not merely delay information. It edits it. On the ground: the customer is confused and about to leave. One layer up: some adoption friction. Two layers up: change management is a workstream. At the top: a small green icon meaning everything is fine. Every person behaved rationally. Nobody wanted to convert an operational fact into an executive's bad afternoon.

---

*The information moves upward while reality is removed for aerodynamics.*

---

The customer, meanwhile, already left.

## Command latency in bad times

> *Command Latency is the interval between reality changing and the person closest to reality being permitted to respond.*

Research on firms entering the Great Recession found that companies which had delegated more authority to local plant managers beforehand performed better in the sectors hit hardest, where local information became especially valuable.[88]

Structure built before the shock determines which knowledge can be used during it. A company cannot improvise judgment after years of training managers to wait. The PowerPoint says, "Take ownership." The promotion system says, "Do not be the last name in the email chain."

In transformation programs, I have watched reversible decisions make pilgrimages through governance. A local deviation triggers an impact assessment; architecture requests security review; security requests legal interpretation; legal requests sponsorship. The customer chooses another vendor while the approval packet learns to circulate.[89]

Jeff Bezos's one-way-door and two-way-door distinction supplies a useful shorthand: irreversible choices deserve broad judgment; reversible choices belong with people who can observe and roll back the result.[90]

The absurdity is applying one-way-door ceremony to decisions whose entire virtue is reversibility. Decide the boundary during calm: what is reversible, what blast radius requires escalation, what triggers rollback, and which ethical limits never bend. Authority assigned before shock becomes speed during shock. "Empowerment" announced during the emergency is permission arriving after the fire department.

## The headquarters-offline drill

Run it as a drill, not a metaphor. First, on paper, remove the CEO for ninety days. What stops? Then, for real, remove the normal escalation path from one bounded operation for one day. Record which decisions halt, which knowledge cannot be found, and which customer relationships depend on personal intervention. Every item on the list is a leg wired directly to the head.

Then publish the list internally. The org chart will be repaired by half the org out of embarrassment before the next drill is scheduled.

The CEO is not the person who knows most. The role is to make purpose clear, allocate existential resources, protect truth, establish boundaries, and let whoever knows most about the immediate problem act intelligently. One boundary deserves its own sentence in the AI era: decentralized action without observability, evaluation, escalation, and stop authority is not mission command. It is unattended automation.

## The Molt

Niches can become prisons, and decentralization can become local empire. Refuse the incumbent's preferred contest only while customers still value the crevice; centralize enough purpose, standards, and truth that distributed action remains one organism.

> **Cockroach Test**—*Which reversible decision is closest to reality yet still waiting for headquarters? Count the days it has waited. That number is your command latency—and your competitor's head start.*

---

*Fabius won by declining the battle. Your board calls that cowardice right up until the quarter it starts calling it genius.*

---

# Killable Bets: Small, Smart, Cheap, and Many

. . .

The beautiful canoe contains the finest materials, the most advanced design, and a steering committee representing every stakeholder except water.

It does not float.

---

*The unicorn builds the beautiful canoe for a calm, open ocean.*
*The cockroach builds a compressible vessel for the narrow gap behind the refrigerator.*

---

The modern organization builds experiments too expensive to admit they failed. The beautiful canoe appears as the global ERP meant to harmonize every business unit and historical grievance, the data lake expected to emit insight after governance completes its migration, the foundation model selected before the use cases, or the transformation whose benefits begin in Year Six.[92]

These projects are not wrong because they are large. Some systems require integration and scale. The danger is irreversibility combined with uncertainty.

## Killable bets

Even the world's most committed empire noticed the problem. The U.S. Department of Defense launched Replicator to accelerate fielding of large numbers of all-domain attritable autonomous systems—affordable and scalable enough that commanders could tolerate greater risk of losing the system.[91]

War has given humanity many terrible words. Attritable is one of the few that may improve a board meeting—and it applies to systems, experiments, modules, channels, and bets, never to people.

Make ideas cheap to kill. Never make people cheap to discard.

Because expensive ideas rarely die honestly. A $500,000 experiment looks tentative. A $50 million program looks strategic. Capitalized cost creates an asset. Headcount creates a constituency. Vendor contracts create milestones. Executive sponsorship creates reputation. Soon continuing is called prudence and stopping is called waste. Sunk cost is not stored evidence. It is money that has already voted and left the building.

## Three exposures, not one

Killable experimentation bounds uncertainty on three ledgers at once. Financial exposure is limited so failure cannot threaten the organism. Architectural exposure is isolated so the experiment cannot corrupt the core. Political exposure is bounded so ending the work does not require humiliating an executive sponsor.

Most organizations manage the first and ignore the other two, then wonder why inexpensive pilots live forever. The pilot is cheap. The integration is permanent. The sponsor is senior. The conclusion is predetermined. This is not experimentation. It is theater with test data.

## The Flipped Gunpowder Paradox

Now widen the lens, because the Gods have run this experiment at civilizational scale. Gunpowder emerged in China, where Chinese states developed and used early gunpowder weapons. Over centuries the technology diffused, mutated, and was driven through different systems of military competition; by the eighteenth century, European states had gained decisive advantages in many gunpowder technologies. The honest history is not the nursery tale that China invented and Europe alone weaponized it. It is the more useful warning that origin does not guarantee control over the deployment regime that follows.[93]

In *Farmer versus Hunter*, I called the older wound the Gunpowder Paradox:

*Invention without deployment becomes intellectual philanthropy—you do the thinking, and somebody else does the conquering.*

**Invention is not deployment. Deployment is not diffusion. Diffusion is not institutional absorption.**

A nation can hold the patent and lose the century. A company can hold the demo and lose the market.

The AI version has flipped the compass but not the logic. Many foundational advances in the current AI wave emerged from American and Canadian institutions. Strategic advantage will accrue to whoever makes capability cheap, ordinary, embedded, and difficult to remove from daily life.

In February 2025, BYD announced that its "God's Eye" driver-assistance technology would be offered across twenty-one models, including several below 100,000 yuan. The announcement did not prove autonomy, and the company's claims deserve the usual skepticism. Its strategic meaning was deployment: capability presented as a premium differentiator was being pushed toward ordinary equipment across a mass-market lineup.[94]

The laboratory announces a breakthrough; the factory announces a million installations. The patent office records the first. History tends to remember the second.

*Discovery receives the patent. Deployment receives the century.*

The cheap, sufficiently capable system does not always defeat the exquisite one. It changes the battlefield by making yesterday's miracle today's standard equipment. Small, smart, cheap, and many is not a startup aesthetic. It is how technological eras become ordinary enough to matter.

## Match commitment to knowledge

When knowledge is low, preserve reversibility. As evidence accumulates, increase commitment. When reversal is difficult or the blast radius large, slow down and broaden judgment. Most project governance reverses this logic: it demands precise forecasts while uncertainty is highest, then treats new evidence as disloyal after the budget is approved.

A useful experiment answers a defined question. Will the customer change this behavior? Can the workflow operate safely? Can the supplier meet the tolerance? Does the model improve the decision after supervision and exception costs? It also has a graduation rule: what evidence earns another dollar, what result requires replication, and what failure ends the path?

A pilot without a decision rule is not experimentation. It is theater with test data.

Many is not duplication. It is variation joined by common protocols and honest selection.

## One enormous answer

England's National Program for IT in the NHS began in 2002 with a worthy ambition: modernize records, booking, prescriptions, networks, and care systems across an immense health service. The difficulty was an architecture of sweeping centralized contracts imposed across organizations with different workflows and installed systems. The government later dismantled the program into components; a 2013 parliamentary report forecast final costs around £9.8 billion, excluding some future costs, and described delayed core systems, weak accountability, and supplier problems. Some components delivered value and continued. The total program had become too large to learn cleanly.[95]

Healthcare.gov supplies the compact countercase: a large integrated objective can recover when failures are isolated and components, contractors, authority, and operating methods can be replaced.[96]

The choice is not one central system or local chaos. Identity, security, core data standards, and shared infrastructure may require integration. Workflows and experimentation may require bounded variation. The center supplies rails; local teams supply learning. "Many" without common protocols is not a swarm. It is duplication wearing innovation badges.

## The Molt

Small bets can become a refuge from conviction, just as grand programs can become a refuge from evidence. Semiconductor fabs, clinical trials, payment networks, and safety-critical ledgers eventually require concentration. Preserve reversibility while uncertainty is high. Commit when evidence justifies commitment. Make ideas easy to kill without making people disposable.

> **Cockroach Test**—*Which initiative has become too prestigious, integrated, or career-defining to fail honestly? Name the evidence that would kill it—and ask whether anyone is allowed to collect that evidence.*

Build canoes that float or experiments that sink quietly. The unforgivable vessel takes the whole crew down while the steering committee is still arguing about the color of the life jackets.

---

*If a project is too big to fail, it is too dangerous to launch.*

*A fifty-million-dollar failure is never called a failure. It is called "Phase One of a multi-year capability realignment." Sunk cost isn't an economic fallacy in the enterprise; it's a corporate defense mechanism designed to protect the executive who signed the initial purchase order.*

---

# Cockroaches Check the Pantry

. . .

Every strategy is a supply request wearing a better suit.

On March 11, 2011, the earthquake and tsunami in northeastern Japan killed thousands, devastated communities, disrupted power and transport, and fractured industrial networks whose complexity became visible only when parts stopped arriving. Toyota suspended production and spent the following weeks tracing inventories, suppliers, and components that might take months to recover.[97]

Critics reached for a familiar verdict: just-in-time had finally met reality. Reality was less convenient. The vulnerability was not simply low inventory. It was a deep multi-tier network containing concentrations and dependencies whose location and substitutability were not fully visible from the center. Strategy did not fail at the level of vision. It failed where strategy always becomes real: somebody could not obtain the part.

## Nouns are lighter than trucks

The optimized company assigns the pantry to functions. Procurement owns supply, IT owns systems, HR owns skill, Legal owns permission, Finance owns cash, and Communications owns trust—a wonderfully efficient way to ensure nobody owns the system. Winter ignores the org chart. A cyberattack becomes a port delay; a missing component becomes a refund; a cash shortage becomes a quality problem; a burned-out maintainer becomes an outage.

The pantry—parts, power, transport, data, code, backups, skill, certification, permits, insurance, cash, credit, supplier trust, customer patience—fails as a system.

Growth requests working capital. AI requests electricity, chips, model access, data quality, supervision, and customer permission. International expansion requests tax registration, logistics, foreign exchange, local trust, and government cooperation. The strategy deck can conceal these requests because nouns are lighter than trucks.

Military organizations call the systems that keep operations possible sustainment. Contemporary Army writing on contested logistics dwells on routes, nodes, fuel, ports, and information systems for one reason: an adversary attacks what the plan depends upon.[98]

Markets are not battlefields. The transferable lesson is that what management calls support may be the system's most concentrated source of power—and fragility.

---

*Your twenty-four-year-old product manager thinks his code is weightless, blissfully unaware that his software requires diesel fuel, a Taiwanese fab, and the U.S. Navy to function.*

---

Your "optimized, asset-light" supply chain is actually just a heavy reliance on permanent global peace, which historically has the lifespan of a fruit fly. Agile methodology is entirely useless if two guys with consumer drones in the Red Sea decide to cancel your fiscal year.

## Toyota maps the invisible tiers

Toyota did not answer 2011 by filling Japan with inventory. It invested in visibility, recovery, coordination, and continuity. By 2016 the company described a supply-chain database called RESCUE containing information on approximately 6,800 items, supported by supplier training and standardized information.[99]

Inventory buys time. So do visibility, a qualified substitute, a documented recovery sequence, and a supplier relationship strong enough to produce bad news early. A database cannot manufacture a missing semiconductor or repeal geography. It can shorten the interval between disruption and comprehension—often the only interval management still controls.

## Maersk and the digital supply line

On June 27, 2017, NotPetya spread through networks worldwide. Maersk was among the major victims; systems affecting container shipping, terminals, and logistics were disrupted, and the company estimated a $200–300 million negative impact.[100]

The event is usually filed under cybersecurity. It was also logistics. Maersk could possess ships, containers, cranes, contracts, and customers while discovering that the information coordinating them had become part of the physical supply line. The attack did not need to sink a vessel. It interfered with the knowledge required to move one.

## The pantry has acquired a passport

Now open the cupboard the org chart never audits. For every load-bearing input, ask: where was it made? Under whose export rules? Through which port or strait? Insured by whom, and does the insurer still cover the route? Priced in which currency? Hosted on whose cloud? Running whose model? Powered by which grid?

What happens when two governments stop agreeing that the transaction should exist?

During the 2026 conflict involving Iran, traffic through the Strait of Hormuz repeatedly collapsed, partially resumed, and fell again as attacks, restrictions, insurance withdrawal, blockades, and negotiations changed the operating environment. The precise flow depended on the date and tracker. The structural fact did not: a route that before the war carried roughly one-fifth of global oil and LNG shipments became a live political dependency.[101]

Companies with no office near the Gulf and no public position on the conflict discovered that their pantry had a foreign policy: freight surcharges, energy costs, delayed components, insurance exclusions, and a CFO learning the word demurrage.

The response is not autarky. No company can onshore the planet. It is conscious dependence: know which geopolitical input can kill you, how fast, what substitution costs, and what will happen during the interval.

---

*A single-strait supply line is a single point of failure that happens to have a navy.*

---

## Design the degraded company

Define the least capable version of the firm that can still protect people, preserve trust, create value, and earn revenue. Not every feature, market, or service level—the irreducible service. For an AI company, that may mean a smaller model, slower turnaround, deterministic fallback, or human review. For a manufacturer, a reduced product mix. For a professional-services firm, delivery without the elegant internal platform that was supposed to eliminate email and instead invented six new kinds of it.

---

*Define the irreducible service.*
*Name the three pantry items without which it cannot be delivered.*
*Pre-authorize the trigger that moves the organization into degraded mode.*

---

Degraded mode changes with time. A manual workaround that functions for four hours may collapse after four days. First hour, first day, first week, first month: sleep, attention, cash, spare parts, customer patience, and regulatory tolerance become scarce on different calendars. The plan must specify the quality floor that does not fall with them.

An emergency response that preserves revenue by exporting risk to customers is not resilience. It is a transfer. And a recovery plan never exercised is a forecast wearing a high-visibility vest. Operate briefly without the preferred system before the preferred system chooses the date.

In aerospace and defense work, grand strategy eventually meets the inventory list. Extraordinary engineering can still stop for a specialized connector, an export-controlled component, a certification, a sole-source process, or a data interface. The system's most glamorous element is rarely the one that halts production.[102]

That experience teaches humility faster than a keynote. Logistics is strategy with the adjectives removed.

## Cash is the first pantry

Cash is inventory with universal compatibility. Accounts receivable is inventory stored inside the customer. Debt capacity is an emergency supplier whose terms change precisely when needed. Gross margin determines whether each unit of demand replenishes the pantry or quietly eats it.

A company can report growth while starving: orders it cannot finance, customers who pay too slowly, equipment whose carrying cost outruns throughput, or a brilliant product whose support burden turns each sale into a delayed liability. Annual recurring revenue can be comforting while cloud expense, implementation labor, fraud, warranties, and receivables consume cash on different calendars. The organism experiences timing, not the board pack's presentation format.

. . .

The answer is not a bunker filled with every possible backup. Civilization is specialization. The objective is conscious dependence: know what can fail, how long substitution takes, what failure costs, and what the company will do while the substitute arrives. A buffer earns its cost only when it buys time, recovery, or negotiating freedom.

> **Cockroach Test**—*What is the least capable version of your organization that could still protect people, preserve trust, and earn revenue tomorrow morning?*
> *If nobody can describe it in one paragraph, the continuity plan is a press release that has not happened yet.*

The strategy is not what management intends. It is what the pantry can sustain.

*Check the pantry. Check the passport. Then approve the deck.*

# Scavenger Economics: Never Waste a Good Extinction

. . .

Winter destroys narratives faster than assets.

In October 2010, Tesla acquired approximately 5.4 million square feet of manufacturing facilities on 210 acres at the former NUMMI plant in Fremont, California. It paid $42 million for the land and facility, with additional consideration for permits and separately purchased equipment. The site carried environmental liabilities and the residue of an industrial past. It also carried something a young automaker could not produce through vision alone: a factory.[103]

Tesla began Model S production there in 2012. A prior operating system had closed, its assets were repriced, and a later organism acquired capability at economics unavailable during the boom. Scavenger economics is the discipline of separating what failed from what merely became cheap.

The unicorn sees an abandoned factory and asks what went wrong. The cockroach asks whether power is connected, permits transfer, process knowledge remains nearby, the roof leaks, and the environmental liability has developed opinions.

## A discount is not a strategy

*The cockroach attends the bankruptcy auction and buys the empire for twelve cents on the dollar—then reads the environmental-liability schedule, because cheap carcasses contain expensive obligations.*

Booms create assets under assumptions: factories assume demand, data centers assume utilization, software assumes renewal, and startups assume another round. When the assumption fails, the resource does not vanish. It becomes detached from the valuation that justified its creation.

That detachment creates opportunity and danger in equal measure. A patent may be useful or describe a solution nobody wanted. A codebase may accelerate development or transmit every compromise accumulated while waiting for rescue. A customer list without trust is a spreadsheet containing people who would prefer not to hear from you. A factory without process knowledge is real estate with utilities.

Lordstown Motors acquired General Motors' former Ohio assembly complex in 2019 for $20 million and described the price as significantly below fair value.[104]

The factory was real. Durable demand, financing, and production economics were less so. In 2024, the Securities and Exchange Commission charged Lordstown with misleading investors about the sales prospects of its Endurance pickup, including the significance of more than 100,000 nonbinding preorders and the delivery timeline. Lordstown settled without admitting or denying the findings, subject to bankruptcy-court approval; it had filed Chapter 11 in June 2023 and ceased Endurance production and sales.[105]

Two companies acquired discounted former auto plants. One built an operating enterprise. The other became a bankruptcy case. The difference was not the discount.

A cheap factory is not product-market fit with loading docks.

Large assets create a metabolic floor: taxes, utilities, security, maintenance, insurance, compliance, equipment, and pressure to "use the capacity." Management buys capacity because it is discounted, then invents demand to justify owning it. The asset no longer serves the strategy; the strategy becomes a service organization for the asset.

---

*The scavenger does not survive because it consumes everything dead.*

*It survives because it can digest what it consumes.*

---

## Buy the capability, not the miracle load

Winter destroys ownership claims faster than it destroys capability.

The fiber outlived the dot-coms; the railway outlived the promoters; the Fremont plant outlived two automakers before Tesla drove in. When the current AI boom reprices—and every boom eventually does—the GPUs, substations, interconnection agreements, fitted-out data halls, evaluation harnesses, and trained teams will not evaporate. Their owners may change, at prices set by whoever kept cash and nerve.

Run the depreciation honestly because the salvage table is not flat. Steel, land, power infrastructure, and grid interconnections operate on decade clocks. Silicon depreciates like fish: a frontier GPU is a miracle for a few years, a bargain for a few more, and a space heater thereafter. Models rot faster. Customer trust depreciates on whatever schedule the last incident set.

A scavenger who prices every layer at the same discount has not found a bargain. It has bought a weighted average of a cathedral and a fish market.

---

*...and fish markets do not age well. You are buying the dead unicorn's organs. Do not accidentally adopt the disease that killed it.*

---

Buying a failed competitor's software code without understanding why the market rejected it is like buying a used parachute from a guy who just broke both his legs. Scavenging is a highly profitable business model. Necromancy is a mental illness. Know the difference before you bid.

Before buying the remains, ask four questions. Usefulness: does this solve a current customer problem, or commemorate somebody else's ambition? Operability: can we run, maintain, secure, and staff it after the seller's experts leave? Obligation: which liabilities, contracts, contamination, licenses, and dependencies transfer with it? Integration: is migration and management attention cheaper than rebuilding the capability?

---

*The purchase price is admission. A bargain can be so cheap that due diligence feels insulting.*

*That is usually when due diligence becomes most valuable.*

---

## Pray for the winter—without praying for the suffering

The prepared organism does not celebrate collapse. It prepares for repricing. Winter clears tourists from the field. Rents fall. Talent circulates. Assets return to prices less dependent on permanent applause. Discipline stops being a personality flaw and becomes a competitive advantage.

The prepared company maintains a shopping list before the auction: capabilities it would acquire, dependencies it would refuse, obligations it can absorb, and prices at which the asset becomes useful rather than merely cheap. Hope is not a sourcing strategy. Neither is schadenfreude.

## Slack and the tool inside the failed game

In 2012 Stewart Butterfield concluded that Glitch, the online game his company had spent years building, could not become a viable business. The team shut it down. But it had built an internal communication tool for distributed work: searchable channels combining messages, files, and services. That tool became Slack.[106]

The story is usually narrated as a pivot, as though every failure contains a trapdoor labeled NEXT BILLION-DOLLAR COMPANY. Most do not. What made the remains useful was separability. The communication system solved a problem outside the game; the team understood it through real use, and enough people, knowledge, and capital remained to test a new organism.

A failed AI application may contain an evaluation harness; a dead marketplace may contain fraud detection; a rejected product may contain an internal workflow customers would buy. The hard question is whether the useful capability can operate without the customer behavior, subsidy, founder mythology, or proprietary dependency that held the failed product together. Otherwise, the buyer has not discovered a new organism. It has purchased a cheaper version of the old dependency.

## People are not distressed inventory

Downturns release experienced people from companies whose economics failed. Executives call this "talent coming onto the market," a phrase with the warmth of a warehouse-management system. The knowledge may be invaluable: engineers who learned why hardware failed, operators who survived a supply crisis, product teams who watched customer behavior contradict the pitch.

---

*But people are not abandoned GPUs. They have families, exhaustion, healthcare needs, immigration constraints, reputations, and a recent lesson in how quickly corporate promises become severance FAQs.*

---

Ethical scavenging therefore has an operating protocol: provide honest transition and retention terms; preserve healthcare and immigration continuity where possible; pay for postmortem and knowledge-transfer time; ask what should never be rebuilt; and give the acquired team permission to contradict the buyer's mythology.

A buyer that recruits the engineer but ignores the warning has acquired labor, not learning. Knowledge does not transfer like copper stripped from wire. It arrives through trust, context, and permission to tell the new owner that the bargain has teeth.

. . .

Scavenger economics can become an ideology of waiting. The future does not guarantee a carcass shaped for your needs; trust, culture, research, and learning cannot always be bought at auction. Build what must be uniquely yours. Scavenge only when failure has separated useful capability from inflated valuation—and when your organism can metabolize the remains.

*Cockroach Test—What failed asset would become useful inside your organization—and which hidden obligation would arrive with it? Answer both halves. Scavengers who answer only the first become the next auction.*

# What the Arsenal Cannot Answer

. . .

The asymmetric arsenal has taught five forms of humility: choose terrain before admiring strength; centralize intent before distributing action; make uncertain bets killable before making them large; protect the pantry before announcing victory; and distinguish distressed capability from discounted mistake.

These disciplines can keep an organization alive. They cannot tell us whether it deserves to live.

A parasite also chooses terrain. A cartel understands logistics. A ransomware syndicate can post excellent cash conversion. Strategy answers a narrow question: how do we avoid defeat? Part V asks the older one: what kind of institution should remain after the founder, technology, capital structure, and everyone currently in the boardroom are gone?

---

*The battlefield teaches the company how not to die.*
*Civilization must decide what is worth keeping alive.*

---

# PART V

## THE FIVE-THOUSAND-YEAR STARTUP

> *DISPATCH · NEW DELHI · LATE JULY 2026. After India's education minister resigned, organizers of the Cockroach movement declared victory and urged protesters to leave the sites peacefully. The street phase had won a demand. It had not answered the morning-after question: what do we build with this? Within days, the movement was discussing a wider listening tour rather than dissolving into a commemorative hashtag.[107] Victory supplies a deadline. Institution-building supplies no antagonist and no applause. A crowd can unite around a resignation. It must eventually decide what it is for. Part V is about that harder morning: what deserves to outlast the fight, how obligation survives personality, and how an institution earns the right to a second century.*

. . .

---

*Survive only while something worth preserving survives with you.*

---

Part IV armed the cockroach with terrain, distributed action, small bets, logistics, and the unromantic discipline of reading the environmental-liability schedule before buying the factory. It learned how to survive stronger opponents and other people's magnificent mistakes.

That is not enough. A parasite can choose terrain. A cartel can master logistics. A ransomware syndicate can post excellent cash conversion. Nature asks whether the organism persists. Civilization must ask what persists because the organism does.

The five-thousand-year startup is not a forecast and certainly not an archaeological claim about Theyyam or any living tradition. It is a design constraint: stretch the horizon until the current founder, product, model provider, capital structure, legal shell, and management fashion become temporary. What remains are the harder assets—trust, craft, succession, stewardship, the capacity to change, and the courage to end when continuation becomes harm.

---

*The modern corporation asks who owns the asset.*

*The long-lived institution asks who inherits the obligation.*

---

# The Institution After the Founder

. . .

At three in the morning, the bell rings.

It does not ask whether the abbot has achieved product-market fit or whether the revised prayer workflow cleared the transformation office. It calls the community because the rule, rhythm, and obligation existed before the current occupants and are intended to remain after them. The bell has been ringing at that hour, in some houses, for more than a thousand years. Nobody who first rang it is remembered by name. That is the point.

Now cross the street to the ballroom. Unicorns are onstage. A decacorn near the bar is explaining that profitability is a legacy constraint. Awards recognize the largest funding round, the fastest growth, and the loudest disruption. Quiet endurance photographs badly. Nobody receives a trophy for remaining useful in year thirty-eight.

That camera angle shapes what entrepreneurship notices. Saras Sarasvathy has argued for endurance as a dependent variable and for a "middle class of business": ventures that persist, contribute, and compound capability without becoming enormous.[108]

The argument is not that every small firm is noble or every giant brittle. Scale is an outcome. Endurance is a design variable.

---

*CEOs think they are the entire nervous system.*

*Monks know they are just temporary caretakers of the bell.*

---

## The economy between the unicorn and the funeral

U.S. Bureau of Labor Statistics data make the point without romance. Of private-sector establishments born in March 2013, 34.7 percent were still operating a decade later.[109]

Closure, however, is not one moral event. Firms fail, retire, merge, sell, complete an experiment, or discover that the owner prefers grandchildren to payroll. Survival statistics do not tell us whether the survivor is innovative, humane, productive, or merely the only restaurant beside Gate C17.

A healthy economy needs births and deaths, mutation and memory. It also needs a thick middle layer: specialized manufacturers, maintenance firms, cooperatives, regional logistics companies, software businesses, community lenders, and family enterprises that store knowledge too narrow for a conglomerate and too important to lose. To a financial screen, they may look small. Under stress, they are tissue.

In the Fortune 100 and enterprise-transformation rooms where I spent much of my career, we could dissect the quarter to the third decimal place. We knew the margin bridge by product, headcount by layer, and whether a program was amber or merely reddish amber. We rarely knew how much institutional memory the last restructuring had removed, which supplier relationship could not be repurchased, or whether an "optimized" capability would return six months later as a consulting statement of work.[110]

The visible organism was measured. The conditions of its continued life were not.

*A long-lived company is not the objective.*
*A long-lived capability worth inheriting is.*

## What the monastery knows

This is what makes the monastery offensive to modern management: it assumes everyone will leave. Corporations often behave as though the current leadership team is history's final draft. The founder's preference becomes culture, the CEO's calendar becomes governance, and the chief architect's memory becomes documentation. Then one person departs, and the institution discovers that its operating system had a pulse.

Researchers studying Benedictine abbeys in parts of Germany and Switzerland found average institutional lives approaching five centuries and linked that durability to a mixture of internal control, participation, intrinsic motivation, and external oversight.[111]

The comparison has limits. A monastery is not a stock corporation with better robes; related scholarship warns about closure, groupthink, and concentrated authority. The value lies in extracting mechanisms, not incense.[112]

The Rule of Saint Benedict functions as a constitution rather than a values poster. The abbot has authority, but the office is bounded by rule and obligation. Important matters call for counsel, including the perspective of younger members. Purpose remains central; participation is distributed. Authority exists without becoming identical to personality.[113]

## Separate the rule from the furniture

The Abbey of Monte Cassino, traditionally founded by Benedict in the sixth century, has been destroyed and rebuilt repeatedly through war and upheaval. Its continuity did not depend on one building, one abbot, or one administrative shell. Rule, records, practice, and community carried form across physical ruin.[114]

Corporations frequently reverse the relationship. They build a headquarters and call it culture, install an ERP system and call it process, retain a founder and call it purpose. Then the office closes, the software changes, or the founder leaves, and management discovers that nothing important was made portable.

The institution after the founder needs a rule short enough to remember and strong enough to survive desperation.

- *Purpose: Why do we deserve to exist?*
- *Boundary: What may no temporary leader consume?*
- *Memory: Which knowledge must outlive current experts?*
- *Authority: How does decision power transfer before an emergency?*
- *Ending: Under what conditions should the institution close?*

Then make succession operational. Before the next board meeting, identify one decision only the founder can make, one relationship only the founder owns, and one assumption that exists only in the founder's head. Transfer all three.

A succession plan stored in one person is not a plan. It is a hostage note with a letterhead.

*If your company's survival requires your CEO to be immortal, you haven't built a business;*

*you've built a pharaoh's tomb.*

And history tells us that pharaohs' tombs are only good for two things: trapping the people who built them, and being looted by scavengers. A CEO builds a legacy by putting his name on a building. An abbot builds a legacy by ensuring the building still exists when his name is entirely forgotten.

## The Molt

Endurance can become a sanctuary for mediocrity, family privilege, protected monopoly, and subsidized zombification. Monasteries can ossify; missions can become unpaid compensation; rituals can survive after meaning leaves.

Useful endurance must therefore be judged beside renewal, contribution, productivity, and legitimacy. The goal is not to prevent death. It is to make useful life more durable—and useless life easier to end.

**Cockroach Test**—*If the founder disappeared tomorrow, which purpose, capability, relationship, and obligation would survive without requiring the successor to impersonate the founder?*

*The bell rings whether or not the abbot is home. Build the thing that rings.*

# Shinise: Change Everything Except the Reason to Exist

. . .

A construction lineage in Osaka began building temples in 578, before most modern states had settled on a flag.

Kongō Gumi endured political regimes, fires, wars, earthquakes, and the eventual discovery by modern accounting that eternity cannot be depreciated on a straight-line basis. In 2006, financial pressure ended its independence. The operating company, name, and craft continued inside Takamatsu Construction Group; the old family-controlled shell did not.[115]

It is the perfect longevity case precisely because it refuses to behave as a morality tale. It is evidence for endurance and against immortality.

The shell can die while the craft survives.

Fourteen centuries of temple carpentry did not depend on one cap table. When the finances failed, what was worth preserving crossed over. What was merely legal stayed behind.

## A forest of old firms

Kongō Gumi is spectacular, but Japan's long-lived business population is broader. Teikoku Databank counted 46,708 operating firms more than a century old as of December 2025—3.11 percent of the firms in its national analysis.[116]

Set that beside the ecosystem this book began with: one widely cited forecast suggested average S&P 500 tenure could fall toward twelve years by 2027—roughly the term of an enthusiastic auto loan. The forecast may miss the decimal. The contrast still demands attention: a forest of centenarians beside an economy that treats a decade as geological time.

Research on Japanese shinise firms points not to frozen products but to continuity in an essential rationale combined with continuing adjustment to the cultural and commercial environment.[117]

Watch it in one glass. Japan's oldest sake houses have held the family name over the door for centuries while everything behind the door molted—rice sourcing, brewing technology, the bottle, the label, the distribution, sometimes the ownership itself. The promise stayed legible. The furniture changed.

## Hard essence. Soft expression.

In a long-lived brewer, the name above the door may remain while rice contracts, fermentation controls, bottling lines, refrigeration, packaging, distribution, ownership, and customers change behind it. The promise is not preserved by embalming the machinery. It survives because the machinery is allowed to molt.

Hermann Simon's hidden champions provide a western cousin: often private or family-influenced firms with narrow specialization, deep technical capability, vocational skill, export reach, and horizons longer than the public-market quarter. A company may be unknown to consumers and indispensable to an industry because it has spent seventy years becoming unusually good at one valve, fastener, sensor, blade, or process nobody photographs.[118]

Neither age nor obscurity is virtue. Their significance is narrower: long-horizon enterprise is not an exotic Japanese artifact displayed behind glass.

## Identity is not implementation

Most corporate identities are delivery mechanisms wearing ceremonial language: "We are a desktop-software company," "a department-store chain," "an internal-combustion manufacturer." These statements describe what the organization currently owns, not why anyone needs it.

A university may preserve, test, and transmit knowledge; the lecture hall is furniture. A financial institution may help people store and exchange value; the branch is furniture. A software firm may remove friction from a human workflow; the current codebase is certainly furniture, although the architecture committee may require several workshops before permitting its burial.

What promise could remain valid after every current product, executive, technology, owner, and legal shell becomes obsolete?

## Ancestor Strategy

*The unicorn asks, "Who will acquire us?"*

*The ancestor-minded company asks, "Who will inherit the obligation?"*

The first question can optimize visible growth, package the customer base, defer maintenance, and make the company legible to a buyer. The second documents craft, trains successors, protects trust, and distinguishes distributable profit from capital that belongs to future stewards.

Ancestor Strategy does not forbid sale, merger, public ownership, or the end of an independent shell. Kongō Gumi demonstrates why. Sometimes the shell must change to preserve the work. The test is whether the transaction transmits a capability people will still need—or preserves the trademark while consuming the reason anyone cared.

Try the question in reverse. Draft the press release your successor should be able to issue fifty years after you are gone. What obligation did the institution preserve? What machinery did it retire without sentiment? What harm did it refuse to pass forward?

*If the release can only celebrate the founder, you have written a memorial, not a strategy.*

## The Molt

Longevity can become inherited immunity from consequence. A thousand-year origin story cannot pay today's debt, repair today's product, or replace competence inherited only as a surname.

Age is evidence of survival. It is not proof of usefulness, justice, or permission to continue.

Just because your company has been doing something stupid since the Eisenhower administration doesn't make it a "heritage craft". A hundred-year-old company that extracts rent from a captured market isn't an institution. It's a tapeworm with tenure.

> **Cockroach Test**—*Which part of your company is the enduring promise—and which part is merely the current delivery mechanism demanding to be treated as sacred?*

---

*The promise is sacred. The furniture is replaceable.*

---

# The Commons Has More Than One CEO

. . .

A better dam produced a worse institution.

In the hills of Nepal, engineers arrived with concrete. Local irrigation systems had relied on temporary structures of stone, mud, and trees. Because those structures required recurring repair, farmers at the head and tail of the canal had to cooperate repeatedly. More durable infrastructure reduced maintenance—and, in some cases, weakened the relationships and rules through which water had actually been governed.[119]

The lesson belongs above every transformation office: a better asset can produce a worse system. Hold that sentence while the vendor presents the platform roadmap.

Elinor Ostrom's work dismantled the lazy binary that shared resources require either a central state or complete private ownership. Communities can, under specific conditions, create boundaries, monitoring, sanctions, conflict resolution, participation, and nested authority fitted to the resource and the people who depend upon it. This is not laissez-faire. It is self-governance with architecture.

## Federation is not fragmentation

Amul demonstrates the principle at commercial scale. For 2024–25, the Gujarat Co-operative Milk Marketing Federation reported eighteen member unions, approximately 18,600 village milk cooperative societies, 3.64 million producer members, and annual turnover of INR 65,911 crore.[120]

The form is visible: local producer ownership, district-level processing and capability, and national brand, distribution, standards, and coordination.

Silicon Valley's preferred diagram would replace this with a platform. Farmers become suppliers; the center owns the customer, the data, the terms, and eventually a financial-services product, because apparently every platform must become a bank before the antitrust hearing.

---

*Silicon Valley wants to build a digital feudal state where they own the dam, you own the plow, and they charge you a 30 percent tax for the privilege of sweating.*

---

They call it the "sharing economy," but the only thing you are sharing is the risk. They keep the equity. They strip-mined human history to train a chatbot, and now they want to charge you a $20 monthly subscription fee to talk to the ghost of your own ancestors.

Amul shows another path: federation can create scale without converting every participant into a contractor beneath one investor-owned center.

This does not abolish hierarchy. Quality, brand, technology, capital, and system-wide risk require coordination. Polycentric does not mean every village designs milk-powder packaging in twelve fonts. It means authority matches the level where knowledge, consequence, and legitimate participation reside.

## The Kerala tissue

Kudumbashree gives the architecture another form. Neighborhood groups pool thrift, make internal loans, and connect through area- and community-development societies. Official data dated March 1, 2025, reported cumulative thrift of INR 9,286.71 crore and internal loans of INR 28,619.43 crore.[121]

The deeper asset is relational density: knowledge about reliability, illness, enterprise prospects, family shock, and social obligation. That knowledge is not automatically fair. Communities can gossip, exclude, reproduce hierarchy, and punish dissent. But a conventional credit score is not neutral merely because it arrives from a server.

In the Kerala where I grew up, family, school, party, temple, cooperative, neighborhood, and informal lender did not occupy separate boxes because a consultant preferred white space.

*They overlapped—sometimes magnificently, sometimes maddeningly.*

*A system can be difficult to diagram because it is woven.*[122]

## Rules must grow with the resource

A ten-person firm can coordinate through conversation. A hundred-person firm needs explicit roles. A thousand-person firm needs nested authority and a way to resolve conflict among units. A million-member federation needs local legitimacy plus central capabilities that neither devour the local node nor leave the shared asset undefended.

Scaling is not the act of moving every decision upward. It is deciding which decisions become common.

The design principles are plain, even when execution is not. Keep local knowledge local until the consequence becomes common. Use shared standards where interoperability and trust require them. Give contributors a voice when rules change. Monitor near the resource. Make conflict resolution cheaper than exit or revolt. Let the center supply infrastructure without consuming the node.

*Preserve meaningful exit, because participation without exit eventually becomes tribute.*

## AI and the enclosure of the commons

AI has turned this from governance theory into the decade's live property dispute. Models draw on knowledge produced by scientists, writers, programmers, artists, public institutions, open-source communities, users, and hidden workers whose contribution does not fit neatly inside the firm selling access. Those categories are not legally or morally identical. That is precisely why "the internet" cannot be treated as one ownerless quarry.

The machine's diet includes the commons. The invoice often goes elsewhere.

The governing questions are no longer optional: Who may contribute? Who may revoke access? Who may change the rules? Who can audit the model? Who repairs the shared substrate? Who shares in the value created from it? Which uses threaten the resource, and which restrictions merely protect the rent collector?

Enclosure can finance quality, safety, and accountability. Openness can accelerate learning and diffusion. Either can become extraction. A commons is not "free." It is governed by contribution in forms broader than price. Nothing becomes self-governing merely because nobody holds the CEO title.

*The successor to the twentieth-century corporation is not one legal form. It is a design grammar.*

Purpose must survive the shell. Authority must move toward knowledge. Dependencies must remain visible and substitutable. Capital must fit the organism rather than redefine it. Maintenance must hold status. Contributors must possess voice. Capabilities must be portable across ownership changes. And the institution must contain a lawful, humane way to die. That grammar can inhabit a corporation, cooperative, public institution, open-source community, federation, partnership, or form not yet named.

. . .

Polycentric systems can still become slow, opaque, captured, and hostile to expertise. Dense relationships create trust and can also punish dissent. A network is not morally superior because the org chart resembles lace.

The doctrine is narrower: preserve local knowledge, connect it through shared rules, and prevent one center from becoming the only organ permitted to think.

> **Cockroach Test**—*Which decisions need one common rule—and which have been centralized only because the center finds local knowledge untidy?*

The engineers meant well. The concrete was excellent.

*Ask what the concrete replaced before you pour.*

# Customer-Funded Time

. . .

In September 2025, Zerodha co-founder Nithin Kamath did something founders under a different capital regime often cannot afford: he calmly published the bad news himself on the company blog. Brokerage revenue in the June quarter was down about 40 percent from a year earlier after regulatory changes and lower market activity crystallized risks the company had discussed for years.[123]

Kamath also wrote that Zerodha's absence of external investors gave it the luxury of thinking long term despite short-term volatility. The point is architectural, not devotional: management had room to name the weather before financing forced it to perform sunshine.

Every form of capital carries a clock. The strategic question is who owns the calendar.

Sridhar Vembu has described Zoho's refusal of venture capital as a difference in purpose rather than a moral war. Financial investors eventually require liquidity; he wanted to operate a business rather than organize an exit. Customer-funded time can permit experiments on a calendar inconvenient to a conventional fund.[124]

## Revenue buys more than oxygen

Debt carries repayments and covenants. Venture capital carries portfolio and liquidity expectations. Public equity carries disclosure, continuous repricing, and the possibility of activism. Customer capital carries delivery obligations. Retained earnings carry opportunity cost. No clock is innocent. Some are simply better matched to the organism.

Different organisms require different clocks. Biotechnology, semiconductors, energy, aerospace, and infrastructure may require years of investment before customers can pay. Software, services, brokerages, marketplaces, and business-process firms often have another financing partner available earlier: the customer. Investor enthusiasm says the future might be valuable. Customer payment says something is valuable now.

Info Edge offers a useful hybrid. Founder Sanjeev Bikhchandani has described nearly a decade of bootstrapping before the company raised capital in April 2000, just as the dot-com market collapsed. Management placed much of the money in fixed deposits, discarded the plan used to raise it, and behaved as though no second round would arrive. IndiaMART later expanded at extraordinary speed—its founder recalled opening fifty-two offices in fifty-two weeks—then compressed and rebuilt when the economics failed to honor the pace.[125]

Capital bought learning in both cases. It also tried, as capital often does, to convert assumptions into rent, payroll, and office keys before the assumptions had survived enough weather.

## Runway is distance from compulsion

Startup finance defines runway as months until cash reaches zero. Useful, but incomplete. A company can have thirty-six months of cash and only three months of freedom if a covenant, financing milestone, dominant customer, or public narrative makes certain actions compulsory. Another can have twelve months of cash, loyal customers, high margins, low fixed obligations, unused credit, and several routes to oxygen.

Runway is the distance between today and the moment another party can force the company to make a decision it knows is strategically stupid.

Chapter Five planted that definition; this is where it flowers.

*The cockroach is not necessarily bootstrapped. It is difficult to blackmail.*

No single investor, lender, customer, vendor, founder, or market narrative should be able to force a premature launch, predatory contract, destructive layoff, or mission rewrite merely because no alternative oxygen exists.

## Jugaad has an expiration date

India's frugal-innovation tradition is often celebrated as jugaad: recombining available resources under severe constraint. It can be brilliant in the first winter—local, fast, affordable, alive to context. It can also become technical debt wearing a patriotic shawl.[127]

Phase One may use the junk drawer. Phase Two must know when to buy the screwdriver. Revenue should finance the moment when ingenuity becomes engineering, not preserve the hack forever because its origin story photographs well.

The same discipline governs the AI budget. An experiment a customer will pay for is a different animal from one a pitch deck will fund. The first contains evidence. The second contains a deadline.

## The halocline

End the chapter where two waters meet, because this is where the doctrine stops being finance and becomes biography.

In Kuttanad, freshwater descends from the Western Ghats while saltwater pushes inland from the Arabian Sea. The currents occupy the same channel without becoming the same water. Boatmen set their nets at the boundary because life concentrates where the two systems meet.

I learned the capital version inside my own family. My parents accumulated roughly 97 percent of the cost of a modest home before borrowing the remaining 3 percent, at an interest rate they recall near 30 percent. During the 2008 crisis, I acquired two US properties with roughly 97 percent mortgage financing and later refinanced at rates near 3 percent. The same number—97 percent—described two economic universes.

*Their patience was punished.*
*My leverage was subsidized.*[126]

Neither of us chose the regime. The Gods set the price of time, and two generations of one family lived on opposite sides of the setting.

A durable enterprise often lives at a similar halocline. Legacy cash flow is the freshwater: reliable, known, sometimes slow. AI disruption is the saltwater: dynamic, invasive, capable of changing the ecology. The answer is not to dam one current or drown in the other.

Use the established business to finance bounded experiments. Prevent the experiments from poisoning the quality and trust that feed the core. Let evidence determine which new capability earns the right to become infrastructure. The richest strategy lives at the interface—not in worship of the legacy and not in its theatrical destruction.

---

*The boatman does not argue with either current.*

*He reads both and sets the net where the biology is richest.*

---

. . .

Customer funding can become its own prison. Existing customers may reward incrementalism, delay a necessary platform change, or make the company confuse today's invoice with tomorrow's purpose.

Owning the calendar does not mean refusing outside capital or difficult reinvention. It means retaining enough choice to use either without surrendering the organism.

> **Cockroach Test**—*Who owns your company's calendar? Name every party that could force a decision you know is stupid—and the date on which each acquires that power.*

---

*Buy back the calendar. Everything else in this book gets easier once the clock is yours.*

---

# Enough

. . .

Capitalism has a number for almost everything except the moment it has enough.

Open a corporate dashboard, and every arrow points upward: revenue, margin, users, engagement, market share, compute, valuation, executive compensation. Modern management has sixty-seven ways to say more and becomes unexpectedly philosophical when asked to define enough. The word does not appear in the annual report. There is no Chief Enough Officer. No analyst has ever downgraded a company for failing to know what it was for.

Every organism encounters limits. Only institutions can convert refusal to acknowledge them into an incentive system. The modern corporation has built governance, markets, and executive rewards that make appetite appear less like a choice than a fiduciary reflex.

---

*The cancer cell is the other organism that treats infinite growth as a constitution.*

---

When a boardroom demands endless expansion in a finite world, they aren't practicing economics. They are practicing oncology without a license. We have normalized sociopathy by pasting it into an Excel spreadsheet and calling it a fiduciary duty.

It is the boundary at which more must prove that it increases service, renewal, resilience, or legitimate reach—rather than merely enlarging the scoreboard.

Older traditions kept the question in circulation. Thailand's Sufficiency Economy philosophy emphasizes moderation, reasonableness, and preparedness for shocks, supported by knowledge and ethical restraint. E. F. Schumacher's "Buddhist Economics" treats consumption as a means to well-being rather than the final purpose of economic life.[128]

These traditions have contexts; they are not plug-ins for the strategy retreat. Their shared disturbance is simpler: appetite should not receive automatic authority merely because it is measurable.

A few companies have carved the argument into ownership. Patagonia transferred voting control to the Patagonia Purpose Trust and most economic ownership to the Holdfast Collective, with excess profits intended for environmental work. Bosch separates most share capital from most voting rights through a foundation-linked structure designed to preserve entrepreneurial independence and long-horizon investment.[129]

Neither structure canonizes the company. It constitutionalizes the argument over who controls the calendar and what surplus is for—which is all enough has ever meant.

This is still a book about business.

More is sometimes the ethical answer. A vaccine manufacturer during a pandemic needs more capacity. A clean-energy company may need more factories. A community lender may need more capital because exclusion is happening now, not after a contemplative retreat. "Enough" can also become the favorite word of owners who already possess enough wealth, control, and insulation while employees, suppliers, and customers are instructed to practice restraint.

A generation standing in exam queues has heard quite enough about moderation from people who never practiced it.

Growth is justified when it advances the mission faster than it increases fragility and harm. Enough is not a vow of smallness. It is the point beyond which appetite loses its exemption from explanation.

The forbidden number turns out not to be a number. It is four questions.

---

*More of what?*

*For whom?*

*At whose risk?*

*Toward what end?*

---

# When the Cockroach Should Die

. . .

A company has no natural right to tomorrow.

Not because one quarter was bad. Not because capital became impatient. Not because a distressed buyer wants the assets cheaper. But neither employment history, founder sacrifice, nor a familiar logo creates an obligation to feed an institution forever after it has stopped feeding anything but itself.

In October 2013, Mondragon faced the decision no resilience manifesto enjoys discussing. Fagor Electrodomésticos needed another rescue. Its debt was reported at roughly 800 to 830 million euros, and the cooperative network had already supplied extensive support. Mondragon concluded that further financing could not guarantee viability. It said no.[130]

The decision was brutal. It was also stewardship. An organization required to survive at any cost eventually transfers the cost to everyone around it. Employees become hostages. Creditors become denial financiers. Suppliers extend terms because admitting the customer is dead would threaten them too. Management renames persistence resilience. At that point, the cockroach has become a zombie.

Remaining alive is not one condition. Resilience absorbs disturbance, adapts, and continues worthwhile functions. Persistence merely remains present. Zombification survives through repeated support without restoring autonomous viability. Parasitism survives by weakening the workers, customers, public institutions, suppliers, or ecosystems that make survival possible. From a distance, all four keep the logo illuminated. Internally, the direction differs.

A resilient firm uses support to recover capability. A zombie uses support to postpone recognition. A parasite converts the support system itself into fuel. OECD research has linked zombie firms to trapped capital, trapped labor, and weaker reallocation toward places where both could become productive again.[131]

The question is always the same: does support restore self-righting, or prevent capability from moving somewhere it can breathe?

Corporate death is usually narrated as moral failure: the founder lacked grit, the team lost focus, the company failed to execute. Sometimes the legal entity has simply completed its purpose, lost its fit, or discovered that the capabilities inside it can create more value elsewhere. Honorable extinction refuses to treat the registration as the only thing worth saving.

A company can sell a viable product to a better owner, spin out a capability, open-source technology, transfer ownership to employees or users, archive knowledge, help customers migrate, help employees find new institutional homes, and wind down before desperation converts ethical red lines into optional guidance.

Mondragon did not preserve Fagor. It used relocation, retirement, and other mechanisms to reduce the employment shock for many member-workers, although protection did not reach everyone equally. The firm failed. The wider institution tried to carry people and capability through the failure.

Let the entity die. Refuse to let what mattered die with it.

Now attack the doctrine before a distressed-asset analyst mistakes it for a permission slip.

In fiscal 1997, Apple reported a net loss of roughly $1.045 billion on declining revenue. After product focus, restructuring, operational change, a $150 million non-voting investment from Microsoft as part of a broader settlement, and Steve Jobs's return, Apple reported fiscal-1998 net income of $309 million on lower revenue.[132]

Some firms should not die. They should become different firms. A turnaround remains justified when real customer need persists, capability can be reconfigured, trust is recoverable, financing can support repair, leadership can confront evidence, and a credible self-righting mechanism exists now rather than in the founder's memoir.

The death doctrine requires the same rigor as the survival doctrine. Death can be imposed too early—by impatient capital, predatory competition, temporary shock, or management fashion. "Higher use elsewhere" is convenient rhetoric for buyers while towns, workers, suppliers, and public institutions absorb the relocation cost. The doctrine demands evidence, alternatives, stakeholder consequences, a credible turnaround threshold, and clarity about what will be preserved if the entity ends.

I have used the Burning Ghat as a metaphor because fire removes preferred ambiguity.

---

*At the ghat, title, status, and narrative meet material reality.*
*The body is carried through the streets in daylight, named, mourned, and released.*
*Nothing about the ending is outsourced to a euphemism.*[133]

---

Corporations die in the opposite register. A plant closure is not "footprint optimization" to the town losing its economic center. A startup wind-down is not "returning talent to the ecosystem" when employees lose visas, healthcare, and savings. An honorable extinction tells the truth early enough for people to act. The end is the institution's last act of governance—conducted without the possibility of reward.

Some organizations should die not because they are weak but because their strength is destructive. A platform may generate cash by deepening dependence. A monopoly may grow by preventing alternatives. A company may remain profitable while degrading the workers, communities, open-source infrastructure, environment, or public institutions that make the profit possible.

A positive EBITDA cannot answer the moral question. A ransomware operator has excellent unit economics. Ask whether employees leave more capable or more depleted; whether customers retain agency and exit; whether suppliers become partners or emergency lenders; whether the organization replenishes the shared systems it consumes; and whether the ecosystem would be healthier if the company disappeared.

---

*Biology explains persistence.*
*Ethics decides whether persistence deserves protection.*

---

The goal is not an immortal company. It is an institution that deserves tomorrow—and knows when it no longer does.
Sometimes the most honorable thing a leader can do is hand out the severance packages and turn off the lights.

---

*Zombification is not resilience. A zombie company is just a financial corpse that hasn't*
*been informed of its own death, feeding off the ecosystem's remaining capital because*

*the founder refuses to update their LinkedIn profile. If the world gets objectively better the day your company ceases to exist, you did not build a business. You built a racket.*

# From Stewardship to Instruments

. . .

Part V changed the unit of judgment. We made endurance visible without worshipping it, borrowed governance from monasteries without requesting obedience, watched old firms preserve rationale while changing shell, and saw federations scale without one omniscient center. Customer-funded companies used revenue to purchase time. Capitalism was asked for a number it dislikes saying aloud. Then the cockroach received permission to die.

The five-thousand-year horizon removes the excuse that this quarter is the only owner of the future. Part VI now returns to Monday morning and reduces the doctrine to three questions and one drill.

---

*Stewardship decides what deserves to survive. Instruments decide whether it can.*

---

# PART VI

## THE COCKROACH OPERATING SYSTEM

*A resilience metric earns its place only if it changes a decision. Otherwise it is vanity wearing a hard hat.*

. . .

Part V ended with an uncomfortable freedom: the freedom to let an organization die. Most management books would now retreat into inspiration—perhaps bamboo, a lighthouse, or an unusually reflective goldfish—leaving the reader reassured that resilience is important and magnificently unequipped to purchase any.

We will not do that. A manifesto that attacks abstraction and concludes with *be adaptable* has invented motivational fog. The reader does not need another adjective. The reader needs an operating system.

So we return to Monday morning. Finance has forty-seven pages of forecasts. Technology has an architecture containing enough arrows to qualify as weather. Sales has a pipeline number. Risk has a heat map in which every square is amber, the corporate color of plausible deniability. Then someone asks the question absent from the pack:

*How could this company die?*

Part VI reduces the answer to three questions and one drill. Chapter Twenty-Three connects hostile scenarios to six organizational organs, thresholds, owners, and pre-authorized action. Chapter Twenty-Four changes the unit of time and reduces the doctrine to twelve articles. There will be no universal resilience score, bronze insect, maturity certificate, or executive photograph beside a fern. Every number must change a decision.

# The Cockroach Operating System

. . .

At 8:30 on March 9, 2023, Silicon Valley Bank still existed. By evening, depositors had attempted to remove more than $40 billion. Management expected another $100 billion to leave the next day. Regulators closed the bank before the queue could finish expressing itself.

The speed was extraordinary. The anatomy was not. The Federal Reserve later described a concentrated business model, heavy reliance on uninsured deposits, foundational risk-management weaknesses, inadequate board information, failed internal liquidity tests, and no workable plan for accessing liquidity under stress. From 2019 to 2021, assets had grown from roughly $71 billion to more than $211 billion. The organism expanded. Its self-knowledge did not.[134]

SVB had models, committees, regulators, stress tests, and intelligent people using the word *duration* correctly. What it lacked was a system in which an adverse scenario compelled changes in hedges, liquidity, concentration, authority, and behavior.

A scenario that changes nothing is fan fiction.

---

*The board believed it was managing weather. It was weather's customer.*

---

The Cockroach Operating System begins with that insult to planning: resilience is not a report about what might happen. It is a prior decision about what must happen when a threshold is crossed.

The Unicorn Company never built this system, because its operating wager assumed the thresholds would not be crossed. What follows is the alternative architecture.

## A scenario is not a forecast

The Federal Reserve's 2026 supervisory scenario is explicitly hypothetical: a severe global recession, unemployment rising to 10 percent, steep asset-price declines, market stress, and—for relevant institutions—the failure of a major counterparty. It is not a prediction. It is a hostile environment designed to test whether socially important functions can continue.[135]

Traditional planning begins with what management expects: demand, conversion, model cost, hiring, regulation, capital. Winterization begins somewhere less flattering: *Which assumption can we not afford to have wrong?* Forecast-centered management seeks precision. Winterized management seeks survivability under error.

Across decades of planning, consolidation, and transformation work, I have watched systems measure revenue by product, region, channel, currency, and executive owner while leaving the fatal dependency unnamed. Ask what happens if the top customer leaves, the refinancing market closes, or the model provider triples its price, and a room full of exact numbers becomes a seminar in metaphysics.[136]

## Three questions govern everything

Before any instrument, three questions. Every gauge in this chapter exists only to answer one of them.

***How much choice remains?***

***Who can switch us off?***

***How quickly can we recover?***

**How much choice remains?** Distance from Compulsion asks how far the company is from the moment another party can force a decision it knows is stupid. This is runway measured honestly: cash, covenants, concentration, narrative debt, and the calendar of everyone who holds a clock over you.

**Who can switch us off?** Dependency Concentration asks which customer, model, cloud, person, jurisdiction, financier, route, or permission can turn a setback into an existential event—and how many of those switches sit in one hand.

**How quickly can we recover?** Recovery Half-Life asks how long it takes to restore half the useful capability lost in a shock—and whether that is shorter than the patience of customers, creditors, employees, regulators, and communities.

Everything else—Compression Ratio, Miracle Budget, Dependency Ledger, Winter Multiple, Cockroach Balance Sheet—is instrumentation serving those three questions. If a gauge stops answering one of them, retire the gauge. The questions do not retire.

*This isn't a dashboard for the board to nod at.*

*This is the glass you break when the sky falls.*

## Six organs

The operating system examines six organs. The table is intentionally spare enough to use during an actual emergency, when nobody is available to admire the framework.

*Yes, the organs alliterate. Consultants alliterate for the slide.*

*We alliterate for the go-bag.*

| ORGAN | KILL QUESTION |
|---|---|
| **Cash** | How long can the core choose before money chooses for it? |
| **Customers** | What disappears with the largest account, channel, subsidy, geography, or founder relationship? |
| **Compute** | Who can turn off the model, cloud, data, identity, network, chip, or power the product requires? |
| **Capabilities** | What can the institution still do after expected people, vendors, and systems disappear? |
| **Command** | Who can perceive, decide, and act before information expires? |
| **Culture** | Can the other five organs report pain before it becomes a filing? |

Culture is the organ that determines whether the other five are allowed to report pain. NIST treats AI risk management as a lifecycle obligation rather than a responsible-AI paragraph glued on after launch. The Generative AI Profile similarly emphasizes governance, mapping, measurement, and management across the system lifecycle.[137]

A company cannot manage a risk it is socially forbidden to name.

## Five winters, one cascade

Place the Five AI Winters across the six organs simultaneously. Margin Winter forces discounting. Weaker margin shortens the capital clock. Cost cuts remove reviewers and customer knowledge. Errors trigger a renewal pause. Fundraising makes bad news impolite. The founder centralizes every exception. One winter has entered every organ.

Now add Infrastructure Winter: the model provider reprices, a cloud region constrains capacity, data rights narrow, or the grid refuses the date in the strategy deck. The company may be robust to each event alone and fragile to their correlation. The audit does not paint thirty boxes. It traces the causal chain: where the shock enters, which organ transmits it, where a fire door could contain it, and which earlier decision would have broken the sequence.

## Meridian and the green dashboard

Consider Meridian, a fictional composite AI claims company. Its conventional dashboard is green: recurring revenue up 68 percent, retention at 124 percent, gross margin at 71 percent, pipeline at 3.4 times plan, automation rising. Under a simultaneous price reduction, higher model expense, and delayed financing round, its distance from compulsion falls to nine months. The forecast requires five miracles. Four actors hold kill-switch power. Twenty percent compression is possible only by cutting reviewers and customer-success staff who protect quality and renewal.

---

*The dashboard did not lie. It answered a question too small for the danger.*

---

You were flawlessly measuring the cabin temperature while the plane was flying into a mountain.

## The dashboard is a breeding program

Attach compensation, status, and fear to a number, and the organism will learn the number. Wells Fargo's own independent investigation described how aggressive sales management and performance systems distorted the Community Bank's culture; regulators later found that the cross-sell metric included unused, unneeded, or unauthorized accounts.[138]

Donald Campbell warned decades earlier: when an indicator becomes a target for consequential decisions, pressure on the measure can corrupt both the indicator and the process it was meant to monitor.[139]

Tell a branch to maximize accounts, a hospital to minimize waiting time, an AI product to maximize engagement, or a service team to reduce call duration, and the organization will adapt. Whether it adapts toward the purpose is a separate governance problem.

Dashboards can expose variance, unify definitions, and connect resources to strategy. They can also build a cockpit so sophisticated that the pilots lose sight of the runway: revenue stays green while the relationship dies; a transformation completes milestones while capability remains with the consultant; maintenance disappears because nothing happened.[136]

The dashboard does not lie. It answers the question it was asked. The danger is assuming it answered the question that mattered.

## The supporting instruments

The Miracle Budget asks which apparent miracle can be investigated, which real uncertainty can be tested cheaply, which dependency can be hedged, and which assumption can be made irrelevant. Joshua Gans gives formal structure to the problem: when success requires several independent conditions to resolve favorably, modest uncertainty compounds quickly.[140]

The Dependency Ledger records who can switch the organization off, the interruption consequence, switching time and cost, contractual exit, data portability, tested substitute, trigger, owner, and date of the last drill. If the ledger says a model can be replaced in thirty days, but nobody has run the evaluation harness elsewhere, the ledger contains aspiration, not resilience.

These instruments belong in a full-length workbook. The main text retains only what a leadership team must remember while the room is warming.

## No gauge without a governor

A number becomes an operating instrument only when four things are specified: what it means, who owns the response, what threshold changes behavior, and what action is authorized. If distance from compulsion falls below twelve months, what happens? If model replaceability lengthens from thirty to one hundred twenty days, who may redirect engineering? If Recovery Half-Life exceeds customer tolerance, which roadmap work stops?

Google's error-budget practice is the model of a governed number: teams define a service objective and an acceptable amount of unreliability; while budget remains, releases proceed; when failures consume it, reliability work takes priority. The number does not worship perfect uptime or permanent speed. It changes posture when customer pain consumes the room.[141]

Never average the organs into one resilience score. A company with excellent cash and fatal model captivity is not moderately resilient. Average resilience is meaningless when one organ is fatal. The board needs the weak organ, not a medal.

## The Winter Room

The operating system ends not with another dashboard, but with a drill. Put the senior team in one room. The CEO arrives without a deck. Draw one event at a time:

1. *No new financing for twenty-four months.*
2. *The largest customer leaves.*
3. *The preferred model becomes free for competitors and unavailable to you.*
4. *The founder and senior technical leader disappear for ninety days.*
5. *A credible incident triggers scrutiny and distrust.*
6. *The primary cloud region, power source, or critical route fails.*

For each event, ask: What stops first? Who knows? Who decides? What useful service survives? How much time remains? What action is already authorized? What should have been done six months ago?

Do not accept vague answers such as 'communicate proactively' or 'activate the crisis protocol. Name the account, contract, system, person, fallback, threshold, and day. Ask what useful service remains at 80, 60, 40, and 20 percent of ordinary resources. At 20 percent, preserve safety, data, contractual obligations, honest communication, and the smallest revenue-producing core from which recovery remains possible.

Quarterly, the board revisits the top fatal dependencies. Semiannually, the company runs one live drill. After an incident, separate prevention, absorption, recovery, and learning. Corporations often rush the third and postpone the fourth until everyone who remembers the incident has been reorganized.

## The Molt

Cockroach metrics can become the next bait. Distance from Compulsion can reward hoarding; the Miracle Budget can punish audacity; the Dependency Ledger can purchase redundant bureaucracy; Compression Ratio can dignify recurring layoffs.

Never certify the insect. Keep direct evidence from customers, employees, systems, and communities above the dashboard.

Three questions. Six organs. One governor per gauge.

---

*Run the Winter Room before the winter runs it for you.*

---

# The Fifty-Year Quarter

. . .

Inside a mountain in West Texas, engineers are assembling a monumental mechanical clock designed to keep time for ten thousand years. It is powered by mechanical energy harvested from sunlight, engineered for minimal maintenance, and built on the assumption that attention may disappear and later return. The clock is unfinished. The humility already is.[142]

No engineer can know the governments, languages, technologies, or aesthetic preferences of people who may encounter it in the year 7026. No strategic plan survives that horizon. Design principles might.

## The five-thousand-year solvent

The Five-Thousand-Year Test is not a forecast that your startup will survive the Bronze Age twice. It is a solvent. Pour it over the strategy and watch the temporary dissolve: current product, model provider, founder charisma, office, platform, fund horizon, org chart, slogan, sacred initiative.

What remains are commitments whose value grows as uncertainty expands: trust, learning, succession, honest memory, useful relationships, financial integrity, a purpose capable of outliving its current implementation, and the obligation not to destroy the system that keeps the institution alive.

The horizon restores order among commitments. Principles should survive many environments. Architectures should be designed to evolve. Tactics should carry expiration dates. Corporations often reverse the hierarchy: a tactic becomes identity, an architecture becomes holy, and the principle becomes copy produced by Corporate Communications.

## The quarter that belongs to people not yet in the room

The practical discipline begins with fifty years. At the close of quarterly planning, ask: *What would we do differently this quarter if the institution had to matter fifty years from now?* Not merely exist. Matter.

Would we sign the lock-in, delete apprenticeship, exploit data because the terms permit it, retire the system before documenting why it exists, finance growth with a forced-sale clock, cut maintenance to beat the quarter, or leave the founder as the only person customers trust? A long horizon does not make every answer no. It prices consequences the quarter leaves off the balance sheet.

---

*The question is not whether we can forecast 2076. It is whether today's irreversible choice leaves successors room to choose.*

---

Because if your only institutional legacy is an optimized click-through rate and a slightly higher dividend for a Vanguard index fund, you have wasted your life.

## Two molting problems

Nokia began in 1865 as a Finnish pulp enterprise and moved through electricity, rubber, cables, electronics, mobile phones, network infrastructure, and licensing. In April 2014, it completed the sale of substantially all of its Devices & Services business to Microsoft. The public idea of Nokia lost its body; the institution continued in another one.[143]

Sometimes survival requires permitting the customer's definition of you to die.

Kodak ruins the childish fable that incumbents fail only because they cannot see the future. It invented the first digital camera in 1975, invested in digital imaging, and still entered Chapter 11 in 2012 after the film ecosystem's economics eroded. The old business funded the organization; the new business cannibalized it; factories, channels, incentives, and investor expectations belonged to the old metabolism.[144]

Kodak was not blind. It was caught between what it knew and what it could survive doing about it. Nokia and Kodak are not saints and sinners. They are two molting problems. Foresight matters. Acting on foresight before the old metabolism consumes the option matters more.

## The Return After the Investor

My own long-horizon experiment began in Kerala with Theyyam. I have spent years and substantial personal resources documenting performances of a living ritual tradition transmitted through communities and generations. The project looks irrational on a quarterly dashboard: no clean exit, no predictable monetization, and most of the intended beneficiaries are people I will never meet.[145]

That is precisely the point. Accounting is not wrong to record cameras, travel, labor, and storage as costs. It is incomplete if cost is the only category available for an obligation whose intended beneficiary has not yet been born. What the work is worth is not mine to appraise. The beneficiaries have not arrived, and history can handle the review.

## Three horizons

The Next Winter asks whether the organization can survive the immediate shock without surrendering its purpose. Its disciplines are graceful degradation, the Five Winters, the six organs, and the operating system.

The Next Generation asks whether capability, trust, craft, and obligation can survive the current founder, product, ownership, technology, and management team. Its disciplines are succession, maintenance, documentation, learning, and Ancestor Strategy.

The Distant Ancestor asks whether future stewards inherit options—or somebody else's obligations. Its disciplines are stewardship, legitimacy, honest memory, and the future's right to choose.

## The generational counterparty

The Fifty-Year Quarter has a constituency, and 2026 named it. The generation standing in the monsoon holding an insult is not a case study from the front of this book. It is the counterparty of every long-dated decision in it. It will inherit the dependency you signed, the apprenticeship you deleted, the maintenance you deferred, and the trust you spent.

The Fifty-Year Quarter is diplomacy with the already-arrived, conducted in the rain, on terms the dashboard has not learned to price.

## The Molt

Long-term thinking can become an alibi. Leaders invoke future generations to silence people suffering now; families use heritage to preserve control; corporations greenwash extraction with distant promises.

The Fifty-Year Quarter works in both directions: ask what future stewards inherit and who pays today. The Long Now enlarges responsibility. It does not excuse the urgent now.

---

*The clock in the mountain does not know who will wind it.*

*It is built to deserve them anyway.*

---

So is the company this book has been describing.

# THE TWELVE ARTICLES

## OF THE COCKROACH MANIFESTO

. . .

1. **Reality outranks narrative.** When evidence changes, the story must molt.
2. **Metabolism before mythology.** Revenue, margin, cash, maintenance, and useful work feed the organism.
3. **Fewer required miracles beat better forecasts.** Remove assumptions before polishing predictions.
4. **Compressibility beats brittle efficiency.** Shrink without amputating the capacity to recover.
5. **Keep the shell hard and the body flexible.** Protect ethics, safety, trust, data rights, and promises; let structures change.
6. **Centralize intent; decentralize reversible action.** Move authority toward information until consequence requires escalation.
7. **Capital is a tool, not a habitat.** Use it to buy learning, infrastructure, and durable advantage—not permanent dependence.
8. **Revenue is evidence; valuation is opinion.** Both matter. Confusing them is how myths obtain office space.
9. **Price redundancy against ruin, not perfect weather.** Slack with a purpose is an option.
10. **Maintain what you cannot afford to lose before disrupting.** Innovation needs a system that survives long enough to use it.
11. Molt before the environment forces you. Do not trap identity, capital, and leadership inside the old shell.
12. **Survive only while something worth preserving survives with you.** Persistence is not virtue; stewardship is the final test.

# Still Here in the Morning

. . .

The goal was never to become impossible to kill.

It was to remain useful long enough to deserve another morning.

## The purpose becomes larger than the insult

By the time this manuscript closed, the movement that had ended its examination campaign had already turned toward the condition of public schools. On August 15, 2026, Abhijeet Dipke launched School Thik Karo—"Fix Our Schools"—as a campaign of public-school inspection, social audit, and pressure for basic infrastructure and educational quality.[146]

The old insult remained visible. The purpose was becoming larger than the insult.

Whether this was a full molt, a new campaign beneath the same shell, or merely the next experiment remained unresolved. That uncertainty is not an editorial inconvenience. It is the honest ending. The examination campaign ended. The organism did not. It changed objectives before commentators could finish embalming the first victory.

This is not a business case, and the people in it are not props for a startup metaphor. Their demands concern education, work, fairness, and a future not sold in advance; their courage belongs to them. The design lesson is narrower: power supplied the insult, but it did not control the insult's afterlife. A movement born from contempt refused to confuse the shell that mobilized it with the public work now demanding attention.

## The legitimacy aftershock is not one movement

The tinder was never only Indian. On March 28, 2026, the third No Kings mobilization placed demonstrations across all fifty U.S. states; organizers claimed more than eight million participants across more than 3,300 events, while independent verification of the national total remained unavailable.[147]

In France, Prime Minister François Bayrou lost a confidence vote 364 to 194 on September 8, 2025. Two days later, the Interior Ministry counted about 200,000 people in the Bloquons Tout—"Block Everything"—mobilization against austerity and political paralysis. The protest did not mechanically cause the vote; its proximity revealed the same legitimacy deficit in parliament and on the street.[148]

In Serbia, students and residents were still gathering in August 2026, 638 days after the Novi Sad railway-station canopy collapse, holding sixteen minutes of silence for sixteen people killed. The vigil endured because administrative explanation had not restored public trust.[149]

These movements differ in politics, program, symbol, and outcome. This book does not turn them into one revolution. They share a condition, not a manifesto: institutions that remain formally powerful while growing less able to persuade people that the steering wheel is connected to the axle.

No board should read that as foreign news. It is a customer survey, a labor forecast, and a regulatory preview delivered in the street because the suggestion box was full.

## The clock and the crack

In August 2000, Peter Drucker warned that the corporation as we knew it was unlikely to survive another twenty-five years structurally and economically, even if it persisted legally and financially.[150]

The clock reached 2025. The corporation remained, along with fax machines, annual performance reviews, and the phrase *human capital optimization*. Civilization is resilient in mysterious ways.

The structural question sharpened. AI made knowledge less scarce. Platforms loosened coordination from ownership. Networks blurred inside and outside. Open source complicated proprietary capability. Remote work weakened geography. Infrastructure reminded the cloud that it lives on land. Regulation reminded the algorithm that society also has a user interface.

Drucker diagnosed the exhaustion of an organizational form. This book proposed an insect not as its legal successor, but as its design critic.

**The unicorn was not the enemy. The requirement for permanent favorable weather was.**

---

*What can kill you?*
*What can become small without becoming cruel?*
*What survives the founder, vendor, model, regulator, investor, and forecast?*
*When should the institution die?*

---

## The Camel molts

The Camel was the necessary rebellion: reserves over theater, patience over blitzscaling, roots over applause, the Farmer over the Hunter. But the Camel assumes a desert—harsh, scarce, distant, and legible. The Cockroach Manifesto begins when the map becomes unreliable. Today brings Capital Winter; tomorrow an intelligence glut; Tuesday a grid constraint; Wednesday a regulator; Thursday the founder departs to explore consciousness and venture building; Friday the hyperscaler includes your product free with the enterprise license.

My journey crossed both animals. The boy from Kerala learned the Farmer's patience, then spent decades inside systems rewarding the Hunter's quarterly kill. Y2K opened the door; Singapore's four-second silence exposed the cost of abstraction; Theyyam restored a horizon on which value could outlive the person claiming the return.[151]

The company designed for one desert is no longer enough. The next organization must survive regime change without making survival its only purpose. That is why the final word is not resilience. It is stewardship.

Resilience asks whether the organism remains alive.

Stewardship asks what remains alive because the organism did.

## The dignity of the unglamorous

Most organizational survival is unphotogenic: a backup restored; a customer told the truth before the rumor; a second-line manager prepared before the founder left; a maintenance window completed; a model switched without drama; a bad project killed while it was cheap; an employee who says *this number is wrong* and remains employed; a company that becomes smaller without becoming cruel, larger without becoming brittle, or closes before consuming everyone else's future.

These acts are not anti-growth. They are what make growth inhabitable. They protect employees from becoming emergency inventory, customers from becoming captive cash flows, communities from becoming infrastructure externalities, and future managers from inheriting an elegant machine whose missing parts were once called efficiency.

Civilization is held together by acts whose success is recorded as *nothing happened*. The system did not fail. Trust did not break. Knowledge did not disappear. The community did not become collateral damage. The company was still there in the morning.

## Still here

A cockroach does not win because it is noble. It has no stakeholder strategy, moral purpose, succession plan, or mentoring package. Human organizations must do more. They must decide what the shell protects; consciously accept dependencies; preserve truth when narrative is profitable; know when growth enlarges possibility and when it merely enlarges the target; survive without becoming parasites; and sometimes die with honor.

The Cockroach Company is not necessarily small, old, bootstrapped, decentralized, or even a startup. It is designed so fewer favorable assumptions must remain true at once. It can lose capital without losing agency, a vendor without losing the product, a model without losing the customer, a channel without losing the market, a founder without losing its mind, and a forecast without losing the future.

That is not invincibility. It is the dignity of recoverability. Good companies will still fail. No dashboard defeats mortality. The promise is smaller and more honest: do not die because the story was prettier than the evidence, because one person became the nervous system, because capital became the metabolism, because efficiency removed the organs, because the customer learned and you did not, or because everyone knew the risk and nobody was authorized to act.

---

*Become difficult to kill for stupid reasons.*

*And do not survive by destroying the thing that made survival worthwhile.*

---

*Somewhere inside a Texas mountain, a clock is being assembled for people who do not exist yet.*

*Somewhere in Kerala, a ritual crosses another generation through memory, paint, fire, drum, and community.*

*Somewhere in India, a movement born from an insult is inspecting the schools that manufacture the future.*

*Somewhere in a boardroom, a slide remains green. The future is approaching all four without consulting the forecast.*

The corporation as Drucker knew it did not disappear. It lost its monopoly over coordination. What follows is not one successor species, but institutions able to combine scale without omniscience, intelligence without total centralization, capital without permanent captivity, and endurance without worshipping the shell.

*Silicon Valley asks: How big can this become?*

*The cockroach asks the harder question:*

***How wrong can we be—and still remain alive, useful, and worth inheriting?***

# Glossary of Core Terms

. . .

Ancestor Strategy: A strategy that asks what obligation, capability, and purpose future stewards should inherit—not merely who will acquire the company.

Bait Resistance: The tendency of customers, competitors, platforms, regulators, and fraudsters to learn and neutralize a successful tactic. The moat is the rate of useful adaptation, not the tactic itself.

Capital–Organism Fit: Alignment between an organization's gestation, scale, uncertainty, cash timing, and purpose, and the clock, incentives, and control rights of its financing.

Cockroach Company: An organization designed so fewer favorable assumptions must remain true at once. It is not defined by size, age, financing source, or legal form.

Command Latency: The interval between reality changing and the person closest to reality being permitted—not merely informed—to respond.

Compression Ratio: The share of operating cost that can be removed within a defined period without destroying the irreducible capabilities required for recovery.

Compute Sovereignty: Enough economic visibility, portability, fallback capability, and physical-political literacy to choose among compute dependencies before one dictates the product's survival.

Dependency Ledger: A living record of who can switch the organization off, how quickly, at what cost, under which contract, and with what tested substitute.

Distance from Compulsion: The time and optionality remaining before another party's clock can force the organization to make a decision it knows is strategically stupid.

Enough: The boundary at which more must prove that it increases service, renewal, resilience, or legitimate reach rather than merely enlarging the scoreboard.

Five AI Winters: Capital Winter, Margin Winter, Productivity Winter, Infrastructure Winter, and Legitimacy Winter.

Five-Thousand-Year Test: A design solvent, not a forecast. It strips temporary products, personalities, and platforms from strategy to reveal what deserves architectural permanence.

Graceful Degradation: The ability to remain useful while damaged by reducing service in deliberate layers rather than moving directly from full operation to collapse.

Hard Shell, Soft Body: The doctrine that ethics, safety, trust, data integrity, and essential promises remain hard while structures, vendors, titles, and tactics remain flexible.

Metabolism Before Mythology: The principle that revenue, margin, cash, useful work, maintenance, and replenishment determine survival before valuation, narrative, or prestige.

Miracle Budget: The number and weight of uncertain conditions that must resolve favorably at the same time. The task is to test, hedge, remove, or make assumptions irrelevant.

Recovery Half-Life: The time after a shock required to restore half of the useful capability that was lost.

Scavenger Economics: The discipline of separating what failed from what merely became cheap—and acquiring only what the organization can operate, integrate, and metabolize.

The Molt: A recurring self-critique that attacks a doctrine hard enough to reveal its boundary conditions.

Winterization Audit: A stress exercise that maps hostile scenarios across Cash, Customers, Compute, Capabilities, Command, and Culture and connects thresholds to authorized action.

# Notes · Front Matter, Prologue, Part I, and Transition Interlude

. . .

Cold open, "I AM COCKROACH" scene and chronology (unnumbered by design): the June 6, 2026 Jantar Mantar protest details are supported by the reporting cited in notes 1 and 2 below; the cold open carries no superscripts so that the book's first page reads as a scene rather than a clipping.

1. Express News Service, "Misquoted by Media: CJI Surya Kant Clarifies 'Cockroaches' Remark on Unemployed Youth," The Indian Express, May 16–17, 2026; PTI reporting on the May 15 hearing and the May 16 clarification. The text distinguishes the reported courtroom language from the Chief Justice's subsequent account of what he meant.

2. Reuters, "'Cockroach' Youth Group Founder Leads First Street Protest After Arrival in India," June 6, 2026; Associated Press, "Mock Political Party for India's Young 'Cockroaches' Holds First Street Protest," June 6, 2026; Reuters, "Leaked Exams, Dashed Dreams: Why India's 'Cockroach' Youth Turned on Modi," August 3, 2026; reporting on Dharmendra Pradhan's July 25 resignation and the movement's declaration of victory. Follower counts are dated observations, not membership or turnout figures.

3. Edelman Trust Institute, 2026 Edelman Trust Barometer, January 2026. Globally, 32 percent believed the next generation would be better off; the United States registered 21 percent, down nine points year over year.

4. Jeffrey Shuman and Janice Twombly, "Collaborative Networks Are the Organization: An Innovation in Organization Design and Management," Vikalpa 35, no. 1 (2010): 1–14, doi:10.1177/0256090920100101, quoting Peter F. Drucker's August 2000 Business 2.0 interview.

5. Stanford Institute for Human-Centered Artificial Intelligence, The 2026 AI Index Report, Economy chapter. Organizational AI use reached 88 percent of surveyed organizations, while AI-agent deployment remained in the single digits across nearly all business functions.

6. Leigh Gallagher, The Airbnb Story (Boston: Houghton Mifflin Harcourt, 2017); excerpted in Wired, "Airbnb's Surprising Path to Y Combinator," February 2017. The cereal-box account and Paul Graham quotation are presented as reported recollection.

7. Edward F. Menhinick and D. A. Crossley Jr., "Radiation Sensitivity of Twelve Species of Arthropods," Annals of the Entomological Society of America 62, no. 4 (1969): 711–717, doi:10.1093/aesa/62.4.711.

8. Thomas Bourguignon et al., "Transoceanic Dispersal and Plate Tectonics Shaped Global Cockroach Distributions: Evidence from Mitochondrial Phylogenomics," Molecular Biology and Evolution 35, no. 4 (2018): 970–983, doi:10.1093/molbev/msy013.

9. Sheng Li et al., "The Genomic and Functional Landscapes of Developmental Plasticity in the American Cockroach," Nature Communications 9 (2018): 1008, doi:10.1038/s41467-018-03281-1.

10. Innosight, 2018 Corporate Longevity Forecast: Creative Destruction Is Accelerating. The report projected average S&P 500 tenure declining from 33 years in 1964 and 24 years in 2016 to approximately 12 years by 2027. It is a forecast of index tenure, not a literal average corporate lifespan.

11. S&P Global Market Intelligence data summarized in ABF Journal, "S&P: U.S. Corporate Bankruptcy Filings Accelerate Further in December 2025," January 12, 2026: 785 large-company filings in 2025, the highest annual total since 2010.

12. Kaushik Jayaram and Robert J. Full, "Cockroaches Traverse Crevices, Crawl Rapidly in Confined Spaces, and Inspire a Soft, Legged Robot," Proceedings of the National Academy of Sciences 113, no. 8 (2016): E950–E957, doi:10.1073/pnas.1514591113.

13. Toyota Motor Corporation, "Toyota Production System," corporate philosophy and virtual plant-tour materials, accessed August 2026. Toyota describes jidoka, just-in-time flow, and the elimination of muda, muri, and mura while emphasizing built-in quality and problem solving.

14. Paul L. Schaefer and Roy E. Ritzmann, "Descending Influences on Escape Behavior and Motor Pattern in the Cockroach," Journal of Neurobiology 49, no. 1 (2001): 9–28, doi:10.1002/neu.1062.

15. Chen Li, Toni Wöhrl, Han K. Lam, and Robert J. Full, "Cockroaches Use Diverse Strategies to Self-Right on the Ground," Journal of Experimental Biology 222, no. 15 (2019): jeb186080, doi:10.1242/jeb.186080.

16. Ayako Wada-Katsumata, Jules Silverman, and Coby Schal, "Changes in Taste Neurons Support the Emergence of an Adaptive Behavior in Cockroaches," Science 340, no. 6135 (2013): 972–975, doi:10.1126/science.1234854.

17. Jonathan Z. Shik, Coby Schal, and Jules Silverman, "Diet Specialization in an Extreme Omnivore: Nutritional Regulation in Glucose-Averse German Cockroaches," Journal of Evolutionary Biology 27, no. 10 (2014): 2096–2105, doi:10.1111/jeb.12462.

18. Zakee L. Sabree, Srinivas Kambhampati, and Nancy A. Moran, "Nitrogen Recycling and Nutritional Provisioning by Blattabacterium, the Cockroach Endosymbiont," Proceedings of the National Academy of Sciences 106, no. 46 (2009): 19521–19526, doi:10.1073/pnas.0907504106.

19. Qian Tang et al., "Solving the 250-Year-Old Mystery of the Origin and Global Spread of the German Cockroach, Blattella germanica," Proceedings of the National Academy of Sciences 121, no. 22 (2024): e2401185121, doi:10.1073/pnas.2401185121.

20. Stockholm International Peace Research Institute, "Trends in World Military Expenditure, 2025," April 2026. World military expenditure reached $2.887 trillion in 2025, the eleventh consecutive annual increase.

21. Organisation for Economic Co-operation and Development, OECD Survey on Drivers of Trust in Public Institutions 2026 Results; "Trust Steadies, but People Still Do Not Feel Heard," June 29, 2026. Forty percent reported high or moderately high trust in national government, 43 percent low or none, 68 percent believed voting influences government, and 31 percent believed people like them have a say.

22. International Labour Organization, Employment and Social Trends 2026. Global youth unemployment stood at 12.4 percent, and approximately 260 million young people were not in employment, education, or training.

23. International Monetary Fund, World Economic Outlook Update: Global Economy in Crosscurrents of War and Technology, July 2026, doi:10.5089/9798229047999.081. The IMF projected global growth of 3.0 percent in 2026 and 3.4 percent in 2027, with global headline inflation at 4.7 percent in 2026.

24. International Monetary Fund, Currency Composition of Official Foreign Exchange Reserves; Lowy Institute, Asia Power Index; World Trade Organization analysis of trade fragmentation. These sources support the "Who owns the sky" passage's formulation of contested, domain-specific primacy rather than simple collapse: the dollar's majority-but-declining reserve share, top-ranked American power at historically low index scores, and a rising share of world trade conducted outside normal MFN terms.

## Notes · Part II · The Five AI Winters

. . .

25. National Testing Agency statements and reporting on the June 21, 2026 NEET-UG re-examination. More than two million candidates appeared after the original May examination was cancelled amid a paper-leak scandal. See Reuters, "Indian Federal Police File Charges Against 13 over Exam Paper Leaks," July 30, 2026; Reuters reporting on the June re-test; and Press Trust of India reporting on the NTA's security and candidate-count statements. The dispatch treats "paid again" as time, travel, work, coaching, and anxiety—not a universal second examination fee.

26. Stanford Institute for Human-Centered Artificial Intelligence, The 2026 AI Index Report (Stanford University, 2026), especially the Economy, Technical Performance, and Responsible AI chapters. The report records U.S. private AI investment of $285.9 billion in 2025, organizational adoption of 88 percent, single-digit AI-agent deployment across nearly all business functions, 362 documented AI incidents in 2025, and an effectively closed U.S.-China frontier-model performance gap. Incident counts are documented reports rather than a census; private-investment figures do not capture all state-backed spending.

27. Artificial Intelligence Applications Institute, University of Edinburgh, "BBC TV—June 1973—Lighthill Controversy Debate at the Royal Institution," archival video and supporting documents; Jon Agar, "What Is Science For? The Lighthill Report on Artificial Intelligence Reinterpreted," British Journal for the History of Science 53, no. 3 (2020): 289–310.

28. Douglas B. Lenat, Mayank Prakash, and Mary Shepherd, "CYC: Using Common Sense Knowledge to Overcome Brittleness and Knowledge Acquisition Bottlenecks," AI Magazine 6, no. 4 (1985): 65–85; Michael Z. Bell, "Why Expert Systems Fail," Journal of the Operational Research Society 36, no. 7 (1985): 613–619; Ted Senator, "Implications for AI Research: Applying Lessons from the Expert Systems Boom and Bust to the Current Large-Language Model Boom," Proceedings of the AAAI Conference on Artificial Intelligence 40, no. 46 (2026): 39780–39784.

29. The Y2K passage draws on the author's professional experience and prior essays concerning ERP training, legacy systems, Indian technology services, and the term "cyber-coolie." For historical context, see U.S. Senate Special Committee on the Year 2000 Technology Problem, Y2K Aftermath—Crisis Averted: Final Committee Report (2000).

30. Robert Smith and Alexandra Heal, "Microsoft-Backed Builder.ai Collapsed after Finding Potentially Bogus Sales," Financial Times, May 22, 2025. Revenue revisions and sales concerns were reported during an internal investigation and insolvency process; the chapter does not imply final adjudication of every disputed fact.

31. Thomson Reuters, "Thomson Reuters Reports Fourth-Quarter and Full-Year 2025 Results," February 5, 2026; Thomson Reuters, "Thomson Reuters Reports First-Quarter 2026 Results," May 5, 2026. The company reported 7 percent full-year 2025 organic revenue growth, 9 percent across its "Big 3" segments, and 8 percent overall organic growth in the first quarter of 2026. These company-reported results do not independently isolate AI's causal contribution.

32. Stanford Institute for Human-Centered Artificial Intelligence, The 2025 AI Index Report, technical-performance chapter, documenting the decline in inference cost for GPT-3.5-level benchmark performance from approximately $20 per million tokens in November 2022 to approximately $0.07 in October 2024.

33. Reuters, "DeepSeek to Share Some AI Model Code, Doubling Down on Open Source," February 21, 2025; Reuters, "DeepSeek Cuts Off-Peak Pricing for Developers by Up to 75%," February 26, 2025; and subsequent Reuters reporting on price changes. Prices are historical and time-sensitive. The chapter uses the episode as evidence that supplier pricing changes with capacity, competition, demand, and strategy—not as a permanent vendor comparison.

34. Microsoft, Fiscal Year 2025 Fourth Quarter Earnings Conference Call, July 30, 2025; Microsoft, 2025 Annual Shareholder Meeting; GitHub, "Multiple New Models Are Now Generally Available in GitHub Copilot," April 4, 2025. Adoption figures are company-reported and are not independent measures of daily use, retention, or productivity.

35. International Energy Agency, Key Questions on Energy and AI (Paris: IEA, April 16, 2026), executive summary and demand chapters. The report examines rapidly falling energy use per simple AI task alongside rising aggregate data-center demand and more energy-intensive reasoning, video, and agentic workloads.

36. Shakked Noy and Whitney Zhang, "Experimental Evidence on the Productivity Effects of Generative Artificial Intelligence," Science 381, no. 6654 (2023): 187–192. The experiment involved 453 college-educated professionals performing occupation-specific writing tasks and found roughly 40 percent lower completion time and an 18 percent increase in evaluated quality.

37. Fabrizio Dell'Acqua et al., "Navigating the Jagged Technological Frontier: Field Experimental Evidence of the Effects of Artificial Intelligence on Knowledge Worker Productivity and Quality," Organization Science 37, no. 2 (2026): 403–423. The preregistered experiment involved 758 consultants; AI improved speed and quality inside the selected frontier but reduced correctness by 19 percentage points on the selected outside-frontier task.

38. S&P Global Market Intelligence, "Generative AI Shows Rapid Growth but Yields Mixed Results," October 27, 2025, drawing on 451 Research's Voice of the Enterprise: AI & Machine Learning, Use Cases 2025. Respondents reported scrapping an average of 46 percent of proof-of-concept projects before production. The survey concerns organizations investing in AI rather than all firms.

39. Erik Brynjolfsson, Danielle Li, and Lindsey R. Raymond, "Generative AI at Work," Quarterly Journal of Economics 140, no. 2 (2025): 889–942. The study used data from 5,172 customer-support agents and found average productivity gains of 15 percent, with substantially larger gains among less-experienced workers and evidence consistent with learning.

40. Eleanor W. Dillon, Sonia Jaffe, Nicole Immorlica, and Christopher T. Stanton, "Shifting Work Patterns with Generative AI," NBER Working Paper 33795, May 2025, revised November 2025. The field experiment covered 66 firms and 7,137 knowledge workers. The authors disclosed relevant employment connections and stated that they retained discretion over results and estimates.

41. Model Evaluation and Threat Research, Measuring the Impact of Early-2025 AI on Experienced Open-Source Developer Productivity, July 10, 2025; METR, "We Are Changing Our Developer Productivity Experiment Design," February 24, 2026. The original randomized study estimated a 19 percent slowdown; METR later described its newer signal as unreliable because of selection effects and time-measurement problems.

42. IBM, "Embracing the Future of HR by Becoming an AI-First Enterprise," 2025. IBM states that AskHR handled more than 11.5 million interactions and one million transactions in 2024 while the HR operating budget fell 40 percent over four years. In a May 2025 interview with The Wall Street Journal, CEO Arvind Krishna said AI had replaced the work of several hundred HR employees while total employment rose through hiring elsewhere; the employment remarks were widely reported contemporaneously.

43. Stanford Institute for Human-Centered Artificial Intelligence, The 2026 AI Index Report, Economy chapter. The report states that employment among U.S. software developers ages twenty-two to twenty-five fell nearly 20 percent from 2024 and that labor-market effects were concentrated in hiring pipelines and younger workers in exposed occupations. It does not establish AI as the sole cause.

44. Bloomberg reporting in June 2025 relayed McKinsey technology leadership's statement that more than three-quarters of roughly 43,000 employees used the firm's internal generative-AI platform, Lilli, monthly, including for research, proposal, and slide-drafting work. These are firm-reported adoption figures; the apprenticeship interpretation is the author's.

45. The ERP and enterprise-transformation passages draw on the author's professional experience in consolidation, planning, forecasting, consulting, aerospace, defense, and enterprise performance management.

46. Erik Brynjolfsson, Daniel Rock, and Chad Syverson, "The Productivity J-Curve: How Intangibles Complement General Purpose Technologies," American Economic Journal: Macroeconomics 13, no. 1 (2021): 333–372.

47. Greater Memphis Chamber, "xAI Phase One Substation #63 Providing 150MW of Power to Facility," May 7, 2025. The Chamber is a regional economic-development stakeholder; its statement is used as evidence of the infrastructure and the regional case made for it.

48. International Energy Agency, Energy and AI (Paris: IEA, 2025), and Key Questions on Energy and AI (Paris: IEA, 2026). The 2026 update reports approximately 485 TWh of global data-center electricity consumption in 2025 and a central projection near 950 TWh in 2030. It also describes rapidly accelerating capital expenditure. All projections are scenario-dependent.

49. NAACP, "NAACP Sues xAI for Illegal Pollution from Data Center Power Plant," April 14, 2026; NAACP, "NAACP Asks Court for Emergency Action to Stop Illegal Air Pollution from xAI's Data Center Power Plant," May 6, 2026; U.S. Department of Justice, "Justice Department Files to Intervene and Dismiss Lawsuit that Would Hamper America's AI Innovation and Security," June 16, 2026; NAACP v. xAI Corp., No. 3:26-cv-00074 (N.D. Miss.). The NAACP's Clean Air Act allegations, Mississippi's permitting position, xAI's position, and the federal intervention were contested in pending proceedings as of the manuscript freeze. Turbine counts and operating status changed during the dispute.

50. David Cahn, "AI's $600B Question," Sequoia Capital, June 20, 2024; later Sequoia commentary updating the scenario; Goldman Sachs, Top of Mind, no. 129, "Gen AI: Too Much Spend, Too Little Benefit?" June 25, 2024. These are investor theses and scenarios rather than neutral measurements.

51. Andrew Odlyzko, "Data Networks Are Lightly Utilized, and Will Stay That Way," Review of Network Economics 2, no. 3 (2003): 210–237; Christiaan Hogendorn, "Excessive(?) Entry of National Telecom Networks, 1990–2001," Telecommunications Policy 35, no. 11 (2011): 920–932. The sources complicate the popular dark-fiber morality tale by distinguishing physical headroom from financing, lease, and swap excess.

# Notes · Part III · Excommunicating the Elites

. . .

52. Will Gornall and Ilya A. Strebulaev, "Squaring Venture Capital Valuations with Reality," Journal of Financial Economics 135, no. 1 (2020): 120–143, doi:10.1016/j.jfineco.2018.04.015. Their estimates apply a valuation model to contractual terms disclosed for 135 U.S. unicorns; they are not audited determinations of intrinsic value.

53. The We Company, Registration Statement on Form S-1, filed August 14, 2019, SEC Accession No. 0001193125-19-220499; Angela Moon and Greg Roumeliotis, "SoftBank to Invest Additional $2 Billion in WeWork," Reuters, January 7, 2019; Anirban Sen, "WeWork Throws in the Towel on Its Ill-Fated IPO," Reuters, September 30, 2019. The filing reported 2018 revenue of approximately $1.82 billion and a net loss of approximately $1.61 billion and disclosed lease obligations, related-party transactions, and governance arrangements.

54. Moderna Therapeutics, "Moderna Closes $500 Million Equity Financing," February 1, 2018; Moderna, Inc., Registration Statement on Form S-1, filed November 9, 2018, and final prospectus filed December 7, 2018. Pipeline counts and financing figures are company-reported or SEC-filed as of those dates.

55. Dana Kanze, Laura Huang, Mark A. Conley, and E. Tory Higgins, "We Ask Men to Win and Women Not to Lose: Closing the Gender Gap in Startup Funding," Academy of Management Journal 61, no. 2 (2018): 586–614, doi:10.5465/amj.2016.1215.

56. Jeffrey Katzenberg and Meg Whitman, "An Open Letter to the Employees, Investors, and Partners Who Believed in Quibi and Made This Business Possible," October 21, 2020; contemporaneous reporting widely cited approximately $1.75 billion in financing. Returned-capital and asset-sale descriptions derive from company statements and contemporary reporting.

57. William R. Kerr, Josh Lerner, and Antoinette Schoar, "The Consequences of Entrepreneurial Finance: Evidence from Angel Financings," Review of Financial Studies 27, no. 1 (2014): 20–55, doi:10.1093/rfs/hhr098.

58. Intuit Inc., Form 10-K for the fiscal year ended July 31, 2023, Note 7, "Business Combinations." Intuit reported total Mailchimp acquisition consideration of $12.0 billion. Claims that Mailchimp lacked outside equity derive from company and founder accounts.

59. Blake Jackson and Ilya A. Strebulaev, "Human Capital in Venture Capital: Evidence From 100,000 Venture Capitalists," NBER Working Paper 35501, July 2026, doi:10.3386/w35501. The working paper reports that among VCs with recorded investments, fewer than 40 percent were ever credited with a successful investment and 5 percent generated 90 percent of investment profits. The authors disclose relevant professional relationships.

60. Paul A. Gompers, Will Gornall, Steven N. Kaplan, and Ilya A. Strebulaev, "How Do Venture Capitalists Make Decisions?" Journal of Financial Economics 135, no. 1 (2020): 169–190, doi:10.1016/j.jfineco.2019.06.011.

61. Diane Mulcahy, Bill Weeks, and Harold S. Bradley, We Have Met the Enemy... and He Is Us: Lessons from Twenty Years of the Kauffman Foundation's Investments in Venture Capital Funds and the Triumph of Hope over Experience (Ewing Marion Kauffman Foundation, 2012). The report reflects one limited partner's portfolio, not every fund or vintage.

62. Saras D. Sarasvathy, "Causation and Effectuation: Toward a Theoretical Shift from Economic Inevitability to Entrepreneurial Contingency," Academy of Management Review 26, no. 2 (2001): 243–263, doi:10.5465/amr.2001.4378020.

63. Rakesh Khurana, From Higher Aims to Hired Hands: The Social Transformation of American Business Schools and the Unfulfilled Promise of Management as a Profession (Princeton University Press, 2007).

64. Daron Acemoglu, Alex He, and Daniel le Maire, "Eclipse of Rent-Sharing: The Effects of Managers' Business Education on Wages and the Labor Share in the US and Denmark," NBER Working Paper 29874, March 2022, doi:10.3386/w29874. The findings concern specific U.S. and Danish settings and do not establish that every business graduate produces these outcomes.

65. Sumantra Ghoshal, "Bad Management Theories Are Destroying Good Management Practices," Academy of Management Learning & Education 4, no. 1 (2005): 75–91, doi:10.5465/AMLE.2005.16132558.

66. Consumer Financial Protection Bureau, "Consumer Financial Protection Bureau Fines Wells Fargo $100 Million for Widespread Illegal Practice of Secretly Opening Unauthorized Accounts," September 8, 2016. The "more than two million" figure refers to potentially unauthorized accounts identified in the bank's analysis at that time; later reviews revised account estimates.

67. The Singapore, "Four Seconds," later-performance, and thank-you-plaque passages derive from the author's professional recollections and prior manuscripts, including "Four Seconds I Couldn't Forget."

68. Organisation for Economic Co-operation and Development, Digital Government Outlook 2026: From Foundations to Transformational Impact (OECD Publishing, 2026), chapter "Governing Digital Investment and Capabilities to Deliver at Scale," doi:10.1787/0496b2bc-en. The report concerns public institutions; its application to corporations is an inference.

69. U.S. Department of Justice, "Justice Department Announces Resolution of Criminal and Civil Investigations into McKinsey & Company's Work with Purdue Pharma L.P.; Former McKinsey Senior Partner Charged with Obstruction of Justice," December 13, 2024. The resolution totaled $650 million, included a five-year deferred-prosecution agreement, and concerned specified conduct; it should not be generalized to all consulting work.

70. U.S. Department of Justice, U.S. Attorney's Office for the Western District of Virginia, "Former Senior Partner at McKinsey & Company Sentenced," May 23, 2025. Martin Elling received six months in federal prison, two years of supervised release, 1,000 hours of community service, and a $40,000 fine after pleading guilty to obstruction of justice.

71. Nicholas Bloom, Benn Eifert, Aprajit Mahajan, David McKenzie, and John Roberts, "Does Management Matter? Evidence from India," Quarterly Journal of Economics 128, no. 1 (2013): 1–51, doi:10.1093/qje/qjs044.

72. Toyota Motor North America, "Toyota Production Techniques Boost Home Reconstruction in New Orleans," June 29, 2011; Toyota Motor North America, "Celebrating 30 Years of the Toyota Production System Support Center," March 24, 2023. Performance figures are company-reported.

73. Edelman Trust Institute, 2026 Edelman Trust Barometer, global report and January 2026 release. Edelman reported 64 percent trust in business versus 53 percent in government and described business as more ethical and competent than the other institutions measured. The survey covered 33,938 respondents across 28 countries; it is a proprietary global survey, not an official statistic.

74. U.S. Securities and Exchange Commission, In the Matter of Knight Capital Americas LLC, Exchange Act Release No. 70694, Administrative Proceeding File No. 3-15570, October 16, 2013; SEC, "SEC Charges Knight Capital With Violations of Market Access Rule," Release No. 2013-222, October 16, 2013.

75. Lee Vinsel and Andrew L. Russell, The Innovation Delusion: How Our Obsession with the New Has Disrupted the Work That Matters Most (Currency, 2020); Andrew Russell and Lee Vinsel, "Hail the Maintainers," Aeon, April 7, 2016.

76. The enterprise-performance-management passage is based on the author's professional experience across legacy Hyperion, OneStream, and related consolidation, planning, forecasting, and reporting environments.

77. U.S. Department of Transportation, "DOT Penalizes Southwest Airlines $140 Million for 2022 Holiday Meltdown," December 18, 2023; Consent Order 2023-12-11. DOT reported 16,900 cancellations and more than two million affected passengers.

78. U.S. Department of Transportation, Order 2025-12-4, December 15, 2025. DOT provided Southwest an $11 million credit against the outstanding Treasury payment based on operational improvements associated with a $112.4 million investment in its Network Operations Control.

79. Todd R. La Porte and Paula M. Consolini, "Working in Practice but Not in Theory: Theoretical Challenges of High-Reliability Organizations," Journal of Public Administration Research and Theory 1, no. 1 (1991): 19–48; Karlene H. Roberts, "Some Characteristics of One Type of High Reliability Organization," Organization Science 1, no. 2 (1990): 160–176; Karl E. Weick and Kathleen M. Sutcliffe, Managing the Unexpected, 3rd ed. (Wiley, 2015).

80. National Institute of Standards and Technology, Artificial Intelligence Risk Management Framework (AI RMF 1.0), NIST AI 100-1 (2023), and Artificial Intelligence Risk Management Framework: Generative Artificial Intelligence Profile, NIST AI 600-1 (2024). The framework is voluntary and context-dependent, not a certification.

## Notes · Part IV · The Asymmetric Arsenal

. . .

81. Plutarch, "The Life of Fabius Maximus," in Plutarch's Lives, trans. Bernadotte Perrin (Harvard University Press, 1916); Adrian Goldsworthy, The Fall of Carthage (Cassell, 2000). Plutarch wrote centuries later; the account is moral biography, not a contemporary operational record.

82. United States Marine Corps, MCDP 1-1: Strategy and MCDP 1: Warfighting (Headquarters, U.S. Marine Corps, with subsequent revisions). The business application is an analogy, not a claim that market competition is morally equivalent to war.

83. Shopify Inc., 2024 Form 10-K, Note 4, "Sales of Businesses"; Shopify, "Shopify Completes Acquisition of Deliverr," July 8, 2022; and "Shopify Completes Sale of Shopify Logistics to Flexport," June 6, 2023. Shopify reported approximately $1.97 billion of Deliverr consideration and a $1.34 billion net impairment associated with later logistics-business sales. The figures do not establish that every element lacked value.

84. The boardroom observations are generalized composites drawn from the author's enterprise-transformation and strategy experience. Client identities and confidential details are not disclosed.

85. GitLab, "GitLab.com Database Incident," February 1, 2017; "Postmortem of Database Outage of January 31," February 10, 2017; and "How Is Team-Member-1 Doing?" March 17, 2017. The technical facts are company-reported and unusually detailed.

86. Department of the Army, ADP 6-0: Mission Command—Command and Control of Army Forces (Headquarters, Department of the Army, 2019, with current updates), especially commander's intent, shared understanding, disciplined initiative, competence, trust, and prudent risk.

87. David S. Fadok, John Boyd and John Warden: Air Power's Quest for Strategic Paralysis (Air University Press, 1995). Boyd's OODA ideas are frequently reduced to speed; this account emphasizes the cognitive dimensions of orientation. The business application is interpretive analogy.

88. Philippe Aghion, Nicholas Bloom, Brian Lucking, Raffaella Sadun, and John Van Reenen, "Turbulence, Firm Decentralization, and Growth in Bad Times," American Economic Journal: Applied Economics 13, no. 1 (2021): 133–169, doi:10.1257/app.20180752.

89. The approval-chain sequence is a composite drawn from the author's enterprise-transformation experience.

90. Jeffrey P. Bezos, "2015 Letter to Shareholders," Amazon.com, Inc. Annual Report (2016), especially the distinction between Type 1 and Type 2 decisions. This practitioner doctrine is useful but should not be treated as controlled evidence of a universally optimal design.

91. U.S. Department of Defense, "Hicks Discusses Replicator Initiative," September 6, 2023; "Deputy Secretary of Defense Hicks Announces First Tranche of Replicator Capabilities Focused on All Domain Attritable Autonomous Systems," May 6, 2024; and "Deputy Secretary of Defense Kathleen Hicks Announces Additional Replicator All-Domain Attritable Autonomous Capabilities," November 13, 2024. The initiative's military context and human stakes must not be trivialized through business analogy.

92. Saji Madapat, "The Beautiful Canoe," in the author's LinkedIn essay corpus and related Gods Must Be Crazy manuscript material.

93. Tonio Andrade, The Gunpowder Age (Princeton University Press, 2016); Philip T. Hoffman, "Why Was It Europeans Who Conquered the World?" Journal of Economic History 72, no. 3 (2012): 601–633; Peter A. Lorge, The Asian Military Revolution (Cambridge University Press, 2008). "Invention without deployment is intellectual philanthropy" is the author's phrase from Farmer versus Hunter and should be synchronized to the published wording.

94. BYD Co. Ltd., February 10, 2025 intelligent-driving announcement; Reuters, "China's BYD to Equip Affordable Car Line-Up with Smart Driving Tech," February 10, 2025. Reuters reported twenty-one models with the "God's Eye" driver-assistance system, including several below 100,000 yuan. These are company plans and claims concerning driver assistance, not proof of autonomous driving.

95. House of Commons Committee of Public Accounts, The Dismantled National Programme for IT in the NHS, HC 294 (2013). The committee forecast costs around £9.8 billion, excluding some future costs, while noting that some components delivered benefits and continued.

96. U.S. Government Accountability Office, Healthcare.gov: CMS Has Taken Steps to Address Problems, but Needs to Further Implement Systems Development Best Practices, GAO-15-238 (2015), and related 2014 testimony. The one-sentence comparison is a bounded countercase, not a claim that the programs were equivalent.

97. Toyota Motor Corporation, earthquake and production-recovery announcements dated March 22, March 24, March 29, April 6, April 22, and May 20, 2011.

98. U.S. Army, "Contested Logistics Environment Defined," Army Sustainment, Winter 2024. The source concerns deliberate threats to military logistics; the business application is structural analogy.

99. Toyota Motor Corporation, "Five Years On: Toyota's Efforts to Build a Disaster Resilient Future," March 11, 2016. Toyota stated that its RESCUE database held supply-chain information on approximately 6,800 items and that it conducted regular supplier training. These are company-reported practices.

100. A.P. Møller-Mærsk A/S, Interim Report Q2 2017, August 16, 2017, and Annual Report 2017. The company estimated a $200–300 million negative impact from the NotPetya cyberattack.

101. U.S. Energy Information Administration, "About One-Fifth of Global Liquefied Natural Gas Trade Flows Through the Strait of Hormuz," June 24, 2025; EIA Short-Term Energy Outlook and press releases dated April 7, June 9, and July 7, 2026; Reuters shipping and energy reporting dated August 16–19, 2026. The conflict and traffic status are fluid. The body therefore describes repeated disruption and contested reopening rather than a single permanent closure or one unqualified traffic percentage.

102. The aerospace-and-defense passage is drawn from the author's professional experience across aerospace, defense, enterprise systems, and supply-chain environments.

103. Tesla Motors, Inc., Form 10-Q for the quarter ended September 30, 2010, and Annual Report on Form 10-K for the year ended December 31, 2013. Tesla reported paying $42 million for approximately 210 acres and 5.4 million square feet of facilities at the former NUMMI site, plus additional consideration for permits and separately purchased equipment; it also disclosed environmental liabilities.

104. Lordstown Motors Corp., prospectus filed December 4, 2020, and Quarterly Report on Form 10-Q for the quarter ended September 30, 2021. The company reported acquiring the Lordstown, Ohio, plant from General Motors for $20 million under related agreements and described the price as significantly below fair value.

105. U.S. Securities and Exchange Commission, Release 2024-29, February 29, 2024; Lordstown Motors Corp., 2023 Form 10-K. Lordstown settled without admitting or denying the SEC's findings, subject to bankruptcy-court approval, and reported filing Chapter 11 in June 2023 and ceasing Endurance production and sales.

106. Mat Honan, "The Most Fascinating Profile You'll Ever Read About a Guy and His Boring Startup," Wired, August 7, 2014; Slack Technologies, company history. The interpretation of separability is the author's analytical framing.

## Notes · Part V · The Five-Thousand-Year Startup

. . .

107. Associated Press, "India's 'Cockroach' movement ends protests after education minister resigns," July 25, 2026; Outlook India, "After NEET Protests, CJP Embarks on a Nationwide Listening Tour," August 4, 2026. The dispatch attributes the declaration of victory and request to withdraw peacefully; it does not convert followers into demonstrators or claim that a permanent institutional form had already emerged.

108. Saras D. Sarasvathy, "The Middle Class of Business: Endurance as a Dependent Variable in Entrepreneurship," working paper and related effectuation scholarship. The concept names ventures that persist and contribute without requiring extreme scale; it does not imply that small firms are inherently virtuous.

109. U.S. Bureau of Labor Statistics, "34.7 Percent of Business Establishments Born in 2013 Were Still Operating in 2023," The Economics Daily, January 12, 2024, based on Business Employment Dynamics data. Establishment survival is not identical to firm survival, bankruptcy, or moral worth.

110. The Fortune 100 and enterprise-transformation observations are generalized from the author's professional experience. Client identities, confidential details, and proprietary data are excluded.

111. Katja Rost, Emil Inauen, Margit Osterloh, and Bruno S. Frey, research on governance and longevity in Benedictine abbeys, including internal control, participation, intrinsic motivation, and external oversight as possible durability mechanisms.

112. Emil Inauen and co-authors, related work on governance in Benedictine monasteries and its limits. The manuscript treats monastic governance as a source of mechanisms, not as a direct corporate template or endorsement of concentrated religious authority.

113. The Rule of Saint Benedict, especially Chapter 3 on summoning the community for counsel and the abbot's obligations under the Rule.

114. Clifford Hugh Lawrence, Medieval Monasticism, and standard histories of Monte Cassino. The continuity described is continuity of rule, practice, records, community, and institutional tradition—not an assertion of uninterrupted legal identity or an untouched physical site.

115. Takamatsu Construction Group and Kongō Gumi corporate histories; Teikoku Databank, "National Analysis of Long-Established Companies (2025)," March 27, 2026. Kongō Gumi traces its founding to 578; its independent family-controlled form ended in 2006, while the operating name and craft continued within Takamatsu Construction Group.

116. Teikoku Databank, "National Analysis of Long-Established Companies (2025)," March 27, 2026. The firm reported 46,708 operating companies more than one hundred years old as of December 2025, representing 3.11 percent of the roughly 1.5 million companies in its database and supplementary research.

117. Takashi Sasaki, Masanori Sone, and related scholarship on shinise: continuity in a core rationale or identity combined with adaptation in products, ownership, technology, distribution, and relations with the surrounding culture. The brewery passage is an illustrative synthesis, not a claim about one unnamed company.

118. Hermann Simon, Hidden Champions of the Twenty-First Century and related editions. "Hidden champion" is not synonymous with family firm, Mittelstand company, or century-old business; the categories overlap without being identical.

119. Elinor Ostrom, Governing the Commons (Cambridge University Press, 1990), and studies of farmer-managed irrigation systems in Nepal, including cases in which durable engineering altered recurring maintenance and social coordination. Ostrom's design principles are diagnostic, not universal recipes.

120. Gujarat Co-operative Milk Marketing Federation, "Organisation / GCMMF," current 2024–25 figures: eighteen member unions, approximately 18,600 village societies, 3.64 million producer members, and annual turnover of INR 65,911 crore. Company-reported figures.

121. Kudumbashree Mission, "Data on Kudumbashree," data as of March 1, 2025: cumulative thrift INR 9,286.71 crore and total internal loans disbursed INR 28,619.43 crore.

122. The Kerala passage is the author's lived observation and interpretation of overlapping family, civic, political, religious, cooperative, neighborhood, and informal-credit relationships. It is not offered as a universal description of Kerala or as proof that relational systems are always fair.

123. Nithin Kamath, "15 Years of Zerodha—The Risk Crystallises," Z-Connect, September 30, 2025; Zerodha, "Our Philosophies." Kamath reported a roughly 40 percent year-over-year decline in brokerage revenue in the June 2025 quarter and linked the company's long-horizon latitude to its lack of external investors. The body avoids unverified balance-sheet superlatives.

124. Sridhar Vembu and Zoho founder interviews and essays on bootstrapping, private ownership, and the distinction between operating a company and organizing investor liquidity. Founder accounts are practitioner testimony, not independent comparative research.

125. Sanjeev Bikhchandani's accounts of Info Edge's bootstrapping and April 2000 financing; Dinesh Agarwal's accounts of IndiaMART's "52 offices in 52 weeks" expansion and subsequent compression.

126. The family-capital comparison is autobiographical.

127. See scholarship on jugaad and frugal innovation, including Jaideep Prabhu and Navi Radjou, while retaining critical work that distinguishes resourceful adaptation from unsafe improvisation, technical debt, and the romanticization of scarcity.

128. Thailand's Sufficiency Economy philosophy, as articulated in official and United Nations development materials; E. F. Schumacher, "Buddhist Economics," in Small Is Beautiful (1973). These traditions have distinct contexts and serve as intellectual grounding, not interchangeable management techniques.

129. Patagonia, "Who Owns Patagonia?": the Patagonia Purpose Trust holds voting stock and the Holdfast Collective holds most economic ownership, with excess profits intended for environmental work. Bosch, "Company—Ownership Structure and Organization": Robert Bosch Stiftung holds roughly 94 percent of share capital, while Robert Bosch Industrietreuhand holds about 93 percent of voting rights.

130. Reporting by RTVE, El País, Reuters, and Mondragon materials on Fagor Electrodomésticos, 2013. Reported debt was approximately EUR 800–830 million. Mondragon declined further rescue financing and used relocation, retirement, and other mechanisms for many member-workers; outcomes were unequal, and the stewardship interpretation is the author's.

131. OECD research on "zombie" firms, including work linking persistently non-viable firms with trapped capital, labor, and weaker productivity-enhancing reallocation. Definitions vary by study and often use interest-coverage or age thresholds; the body uses the concept diagnostically rather than assigning a formal classification to a named company.

132. Apple Computer, Inc., Form 10-K for fiscal 1997 and fiscal 1998; Microsoft and Apple announcements concerning the 1997 investment and settlement. Apple's turnaround had multiple causes; the Microsoft investment was one element, not a solitary rescue mechanism.

133. The Burning Ghat passage draws on the author's prior essays and personal reflections. It is a metaphor for truthful closure and public acknowledgment, not a claim that corporate dissolution is morally equivalent to human death or any historical atrocity.

## Notes · Part VI, Epilogue & Back Matter

. . .

134. Board of Governors of the Federal Reserve System, Review of the Federal Reserve's Supervision and Regulation of Silicon Valley Bank (April 28, 2023), especially the Key Takeaways and Evolution of Silicon Valley Bank sections. The report states that SVB had a concentrated business model, relied heavily on uninsured deposits, failed internal liquidity stress tests, lacked workable contingency funding, lost more than $40 billion of deposits on March 9, and expected more than $100 billion in additional outflows on March 10. Assets grew from roughly $71 billion to more than $211 billion from 2019 to 2021. In February 2026, the Board initiated a separate independent review led by an external firm.

135. Board of Governors of the Federal Reserve System, 2026 Stress Test Scenarios (February 2026) and the February 4, 2026 press release finalizing the scenarios. The severely adverse scenario is hypothetical, not a forecast; it includes unemployment peaking at 10 percent, sharp asset-price declines, severe market volatility, and, for specified firms, the default of the largest counterparty.

136. The enterprise-performance-management observations are drawn from the author's professional experience across planning, consolidation, forecasting, reporting, and transformation environments.

137. Elham Tabassi, Artificial Intelligence Risk Management Framework (AI RMF 1.0), NIST AI 100-1 (National Institute of Standards and Technology, January 2023); Chloe Autio et al., Artificial Intelligence Risk Management Framework: Generative Artificial Intelligence Profile, NIST AI 600-1 (July 2024; NIST page updated April 8, 2026). The text paraphrases the lifecycle functions Govern, Map, Measure, and Manage; it does not claim that NIST certifies any system or organization.

138. Wells Fargo & Company, Sales Practices Investigation Report of the Independent Directors (April 10, 2017); U.S. Securities and Exchange Commission, Wells Fargo to Pay $500 Million for Misleading Investors About the Success of Its Largest Business Unit (February 21, 2020); SEC releases concerning the cross-sell metric and former executives. Chapter Twelve owns the full narrative; Chapter Twenty-Three uses it only as a measurement-governance callback.

139. Donald T. Campbell, "Assessing the Impact of Planned Social Change," Evaluation and Program Planning 2, no. 1 (1979): 67–90. The manuscript paraphrases the general principle commonly associated with Campbell's Law rather than presenting a disputed slogan as a verbatim quotation.

140. Joshua S. Gans, "Managing the Entrepreneur's Miracle Budget," NBER Working Paper 34850 (February 2026), doi:10.3386/w34850. The paper develops a formal framework for multiplicative uncertainty and distinguishes real miracles from apparent miracles that investigation or experimentation can resolve. The manuscript uses the concept as a diagnostic heuristic, not a probability score or investment recommendation.

141. Betsy Beyer et al., eds., Site Reliability Engineering: How Google Runs Production Systems, chapter "Embracing Risk," and The Site Reliability Workbook, chapters on error-budget policies. Google's error-budget practice connects service-level objectives, measured unreliability, release posture, and reliability work; the business application in this chapter is an analogy, not a claim that all organizations should copy Google's thresholds.

142. Long Now Foundation, "The 10,000-Year Clock." The monument-scale clock is being assembled in a mountain in West Texas; it is designed for minimal maintenance and powered by mechanical energy harvested from sunlight and visitors. "The humility already is," and the organizational interpretation are the author's language.

143. Nokia Corporation, "Nokia Completes Sale of Substantially All of Its Devices & Services Business to Microsoft," April 25, 2014; Microsoft, "Microsoft Officially Welcomes the Nokia Devices and Services Business," April 25, 2014; standard Nokia corporate histories tracing the company's evolution from nineteenth-century pulp operations through multiple industries. The "molt" interpretation is the author's.

144. Eastman Kodak Company, "Milestones" and "Photography History," including the 1975 digital-camera prototype; Kodak filings and restructuring records concerning its January 2012 Chapter 11 petition. Kodak's decline had multiple causes; the chapter rejects the simplistic claim that the company merely failed to see digital photography.

145. The Theyyam passage is autobiographical and interpretive.

146. Reporting on Abhijeet Dipke and the Cockroach Janta Party's School Thik Karo campaign, announced for August 15, 2026, and launched from Hingoli district, Maharashtra: The Times, "India's Cockroach Movement Has a New Rallying Cry: 'Fix Our Schools,'" August 18, 2026; Economic Times and Times of India reporting dated August 15–19, 2026; Times Now Navbharat announcement reporting dated August 12, 2026. Sources describe school inspections, social audits, and demands for basic infrastructure. They continue to use the CJP/cockroach identity; the manuscript therefore does not claim the identity was retired.

147. No Kings demonstrations, March 28, 2026. Organizers reported more than eight million participants at more than 3,300 events across all fifty states; contemporary coverage noted that independent verification of the aggregate figure was not immediately available. The text attributes the estimate and does not convert it into a verified census or claim a unified program across all events.

148. France: Assemblée nationale confidence vote, September 8, 2025, 364 votes against and 194 in support of Prime Minister François Bayrou; Élysée statement accepting the resulting resignation. On September 10, the French Interior Ministry counted approximately 200,000 participants in the Bloquons Tout mobilization, while unions reported more. The manuscript does not claim the protest caused the earlier vote.

149. Serbia: reporting on the continuing student and civic vigils following the November 1, 2024 Novi Sad railway-station canopy collapse. By August 1, 2026, demonstrators marked 638 days since the collapse with sixteen minutes of silence for sixteen people killed.

150. Peter F. Drucker, interview with James Daly, Business 2.0, August 2000, as reproduced and discussed by Jeffrey Shuman and Janice Twombly in Collaborative Communities: Partnering for Profit in the Networked Economy (Dearborn, 2001). The quotation concerns structural and economic form, not the disappearance of legal corporations.

151. The autobiographical compression cross-references earlier author notes: the author's Y2K and enterprise-transformation experience; the Singapore "Four Seconds" account; the family-capital comparison; and the Theyyam documentation project.

# A Note on Method and Sources

. . .

This book combines peer-reviewed research, official records, corporate filings, company statements, reputable journalism, historical interpretation, and the author's professional and personal recollections.

Contemporary events are current through August 19, 2026. Dated follower counts, crowd estimates, market figures, company-reported results, allegations in active proceedings, and unfinished political developments are identified as such. Where the book makes an inference from sources, the interpretation belongs to the author.

The frameworks in this book are diagnostic heuristics, not financial, legal, medical, engineering, employment, political, or investment advice. A cockroach is an excellent design critic and a terrible fiduciary.

. . .

# Acknowledgments

. . .

This book owes its life to scientists who made the cockroach real; historians who complicated every elegant analogy; regulators, journalists, and researchers who left a documentary trail through institutions that preferred euphemism; and the maintainers, operators, engineers, accountants, frontline workers, and second-line managers whose greatest accomplishment is often recorded as *nothing happened*.

I am grateful to the readers and critics who challenged the manuscript before it hardened into another sacred shell; to colleagues who shared the view from inside transformation rooms; to the Theyyam communities whose living memory widened my idea of return; and to my family, who tolerated the cameras, travel, drafts, arguments, and peculiar circumstance of living with a man conducting due diligence on an insect.

The Cockroach Janta movement gave the metaphor a public life I could not have invented and would not presume to own. Its participants are not characters in a management fable. Their courage belongs to them.

Any remaining error, overreach, badly behaved metaphor, or consultant joke that survived the exterminator is mine.

---

*The insects have retained counsel.*

---

# ABOUT THE AUTHOR

Saji Madapat is the ultimate contrarian Unicorn-Cockroach Arsonist. His journey traces one of the most improbable arcs in modern finance—from a boatman's son in the below-sea-level paddies of Kuttanad, Kerala, to the CFO's office of a Fortune 10 "World's Most Admired Company". As a Big Four financial transformation architect, Madapat led enterprise strategies across forty-plus countries. In a Singapore boardroom, he sat in the room where manufacturing jobs were offshored to Shenzhen. When a junior analyst asked, "What happens when they don't need us anymore?", the room went silent for four seconds. That silence echoes through every chapter of this book.

He did not merely observe the Unicorn-Cockroach dynamic from the outside; he helped create the conditions that made it decisive. A Clinton Global Initiative Fellow, Madapat brings a rare dual vision to Unicorn-Cockroach analysis: the deployment literacy of someone who has read supply chains across forty nations, and the narrative literacy of someone who spent decades inside the financial complex that obscures them. He is the author of over a dozen bestselling books and a Kala Sreshta laureate in ancient Theyyam ritual traditions, where a human performer is painted into a deity through trance and fire. That work supplied the long horizon behind the Fifty-Year Quarter; his professional life supplied the confession behind the Corporate Arsonist. He lives on the banks of the mighty Mississippi, still reading the undercurrent between what institutions report and what reality quietly invoices.

Kala Sreshta (Most Accomplished Artist) Award
(Prof. MN Karasseri to Saji & Subhash Chandran(Chief Editor Mathrubhumi))
-Sculpture by Kanayi Kunhiraman

# Selected Books in the Gods Must Be Crazy Series

. . .

The Gods Must Be Crazy!

The Gods Must Be Crazy II: A Rooseveltian Renaissance for Trump 2.0—American Renewal in the Chinese AI Century

The Gods Must Be Crazy! DRAGON vs. EAGLE: The Trillion-Dollar Autonomous Demolition Derby

The Gods Must Be Crazy! Farmer vs. Hunter: Century of Humiliation vs. Century of AI Rejuvenation

. .

# A Humble Request to Review This Book

. . .

If this book made you laugh, argue, underline, reconsider a dependency, or quietly inspect the environmental-liability schedule before attending the bankruptcy auction, please consider posting an honest review on Amazon or the platform where you found it.

Reviews help other readers discover independent books and help this living manuscript improve. Constructive criticism is especially welcome; praise is pleasant, but contradiction is how the cockroach checks whether the kitchen light has changed.

You may reach the author through www.Theyyam.us or his LinkedIn profile at linkedin.com/in/goodtogreat.

Proceeds from this book will be donated to the Mother Teresa Mission (Missionaries of Charity) or similar missions. Thank you for reading—and for helping the next edition become more difficult to kill for stupid reasons.

. . .